D0083583

INFLUENCING

THE

INFLUENCER

INFLUENCING THE INFLUENCER:

The Unauthorized Dan Bilzerian Prequel

ADAM F. HOWARD

I dedicate this work to the Most High who sits above all else, free from the constraints of time, space, and matter. Ever since you blocked my exit, I place all my labors at Your feet. I hope that You will always take delight in me, for You are the audience of one for whom I perform.

April 9, 2020

Dan Bilzerian
Active 9m ago

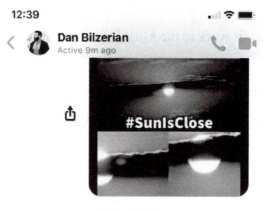

#SunIsClose

APR 09, 4:34 AM

Did you graduate usc, I'm writing my book and since you were my best friend I think you should be in it

APR 10, 4:47 PM

Also why didn't you go to buds in the same class as me

What was the delay for

APR 12, 1:44 AM

Don't be such a woman, I'll sign a Speedo and send it to you

12:29 PM

If I dont hear back I'm changing your name

Aa

Contents

Acknowledgements   8

Introduction   9

1   Great Lakes, Illinois   13

2   Millington, Tennessee   46

3   Albany, New York   52

4   San Diego, California   59

5   Crosslake, Minnesota   105

6   Waddington, New York   116

7   Kodiak, Alaska   120

8   Albany, New York   122

9   Tampa, Florida   125

10   Newport Beach, California   132

11   Albany, New York   140

12   Fort Lauderdale, Florida   145

13   Albany, New York   149

Epilogue   153

Glossary of Terms: 158

Acknowledgements

I would personally like to thank all of my friends, brothers, teammates, mentors, classmates, training and sparring partners, drinking buddies, and guardian angels, both living and dead. There is a little of each of you in this, and this work would not be complete without having known you.

I would like to give a special thanks to Justin and Amanda Greenwood. This work would not be the same without your help. With your talents, it has been polished to a high shine.

INTRODUCTION

Sometimes statements need to be made. This deposition is mine. By giving this account of my ten-year friendship with Dan Bilzerian, I knowingly incriminate myself in several unsavory and criminal acts. I stopped judging myself for my past. I'm okay with calling in an airstrike on my own position. It was in another lifetime. I was never one to burn a bridge; however, I have nuked several of them off the planet.

I'm going on the record and stating that Dan Bilzerian is one of the greatest charlatans of our time. In less than 10 years, he's amassed over 100 million followers on social media. More people will visit Dan Bilzerian's social media platform in one day than the total number of people who will view yours, or mine, in an entire lifetime.

Dan presents himself to the world as a self-made man who has earned his money in private, high-stakes poker games in exotic locations throughout the world. He wants his followers to believe that his fortune is the result of his efforts alone. This, of course, is not true. I call "bullshit" on Dan and his story. I can say this with absolute certainty. As will become clear in this deposition, I have a bird's-eye view on Dan's past that spans over twenty years.

I wouldn't even be writing this if Dan hadn't summoned me in April 2020 to help him remember the details of our relationship when we were close friends twenty years ago. He'd commissioned a ghost writer to enhance his front stage persona and wanted the writer to put a shine on his past by embellishing his history. We'd been down this road before when he called me for material for his cartoon. He used the material I gave him and never gave me any credit, let alone made good on his promise of flying me out to his house in Las Vegas and giving me a hero's welcome. In fact, he never even thanked me, let me know of the cartoon's release, or gave me a copy. I'd sooner burn in hell than do his homework again.

Dan purloined my personality and swagger during our close friendship from 1999 to 2011. The persona he shows to the world is largely a composite of two people: Tom Werth, Dan's BUDs roommate in class 229, and me. The lion's share of Dan's act was slowly acquired under my tutelage in the past. Sometimes the abyss spits something back up. That something is me.

Who am I? I've been playing "first ball in" this whole time and my soul is older than white dog shit. I'm one of the coolest nobodies you'll ever meet. I'm somewhere between *Deliverance*'s Burt Reynolds and a Bizarro Dan Cortese. Dan Bilzerian is the Pierce Brosnan James Bond. He has a bunch of cool stuff from Q, but would lose a street fight against the leading lady. I'm like John Rambo in First Blood Part II where he is stuck on the outside of the CIA jet, cutting away all his gear until he is down to nothing but a diver knife and a compound bow. With only those items, he rescues all the American POWs. I'm a natural born killer of white elephants. I'm not famous. I'm not rich. I'm a rare analog incandescent prototype whose fifth-string, thirty-second throwaway elevator speech trumps most people's entire life story. I'm Dan Bilzerian's negative free roll.

Nobody gets away with anything, and I'm no exception. For the first forty years of my life, I was in a freefall without a chute. Only now am I learning how to put it on. That lifestyle sustained catastrophic radioactive consequences both intended and unintended. Nobody gets away with anything, in the same way that thunder is always preceded by lightning. If it weren't for this deposition, Dan would have gotten away with being an expensive fugazi of me. This deposition will balance the equation and give those who have followed Dan's meteoric rise to fame an insight into where he got his personality and swagger from. Contrary to what he wants you to believe, he is not a self-made man. Everything about him has been acquired. He is one acquisition stacked on top of another.

When Dan texted me in April asking for details for his book, it flipped a switch in me. That was the last straw. Dan had stolen enough of my material in the past to last him more than his natural life. Since Dan has never given me an ounce of credit for anything ever, I'm going to take credit wherever I recognize my influence. If Dan feels that an explanation of our friendship is important to his biography, I will give it in my own words.

1

GREAT LAKES, ILLINOIS

SEPTEMBER 1999

On September 9,1999 I graduated from Naval Basic Training in Great Lakes, IL. From there, I reported across the street to the Great Lakes Naval Station. Here, I completed the basic core classes for the Fleet Navy while I waited for my spot in Quartermaster A School. I spent the first two weeks in a barracks full of gas turbine engineers headed to the Fleet to be push button mechanics. On the last day or two of September, my orders came through for school. I packed my gear into my seabag and requested a ride in the duty van across base to the A School Barracks. I got out of the van with my bag and thanked the duty driver for the ride. I walked to the front door of the nondescript building. This was where I first met Daniel Brandon Bilzerian. He was standing watch on the quarterdeck of the Quartermaster A School Barracks. As I approached the desk, the first thing I noticed was that he wore white socks with his dress uniform. He was reading a *Guns and Ammo Magazine* with a book tucked into it. Without acknowledging him first, I reached over the counter and swiped the book right out of his hands. It was the *World Anabolic Reference Guide* by W. Nathaniel Phillips, aka Bill Phillips, CEO of EAS Nutrition.

"Doing some homework? Making a shopping list?" I smiled as I made eye contact.

"Sort of thinking about it," he said to me, making eye contact briefly and then looking down at the desk. "I've got stress fractures and want to know if there's anything that'll make them heal faster."

"You going to Special Programs?" I inquired.

"Yeah. Why?"

"Me too."

"Are you checking in for A School?"

"Quartermaster. It starts in a few."

"I just graduated. It's easy. What are your thoughts regarding drugs and accelerated injury healing?"

"They're extensive. Deca allows one to recover in what seems minutes. It's very safe. The only negative I know of is hypertension associated with the water retention."

"The book said that Dianabol can put calcium deposits in your bones. They also say it's great for roborizing. That means…"

"It means overall strengthening of the entire body. Yeah, I know this. I read this book last year. How long have you waited to use roborizing in a conversation?"

We both laughed out loud, then I handed him back the book.

"My name's Adam."

"I'm Dan. Good to meet you. You've got to meet the chief," he said.

Dan walked me down to the barracks office where I met Chief Vuketiche. He was the ranking barracks noncommissioned officer (NCO).

Most NCO's on base were overly formal and unpleasant to be in the same room with. This guy had the eyes of a crazy person. I couldn't tell if he was born that way, partied too much, or saw too much. The likely scenario was probably a mix of all three. He looked like an outlaw biker with a clean haircut and well-groomed moustache. When he shook my hand, I noticed that he had the Danzig horned skull tattoo on the top of his right hand. On his other arm was a Misfits tattoo. "Last Caress" played on the stereo which made the chief smile ear to ear.

"Stop in if you ever need anything Howard," smiled the chief as he shook our hands. We then walked out of the office.

"Did you see the tattoos on his forearms?" Dan asked.

"Of course."

"Chief looks like a hardcore guy."

"Well, he certainly likes his Misfits."

"Who are these Misfits?"

"They're a punk rock band from the 70's. They were playing on the chief's stereo just then. That hooded skull tattoo Chief has is a Misfits logo. Their singer was a guy named Glen Danzig. His tattoo of the horned skull is the Danzig logo. He recorded "Mother." That did not register on Bilzerian's face, so I abandoned the pop culture reference.

"How the hell do you know all this, Howard?"

"I was born before 1980."

Dan told me his room number as I picked up my bags. We shook hands.

"Seriously, I've always paid attention to where my elders got their influences. My homeroom teacher in ninth grade was this far out former Ranger and Green Beret. He used to play the Misfits in his classroom. Russ Weaver was a fucking lunatic. He tried to bite my friend's ear off in wrestling practice," I said before walking back to my new room.

I headed out to breakfast the next morning. Bilzerian was standing watch again. I stopped to say hello, and Dan told me he had a strange dream the night before. He said that I was in it. He and I somehow were in an intense firefight somewhere with a bunch of gangbangers. We were vastly outnumbered and were about to run out of ammunition. Chief Vuketiche showed up in his white pickup truck at the zero hour with boxes of bullets and a few cases of beer. He kept us from being overrun and was key in helping us win the firefight.

"The chief awarded us combat medals on the spot, Howard. Then he awarded himself a pair of lieutenant bars. From there, we got into his truck and headed to the strip club where he was a minor celebrity. All the girls called him "the Bad Lieutenant." It was wild man, I tell you," Dan rambled.

Not ten seconds after Dan said this, the chief walked past us. He was headed home for the weekend. In unison, we asked him what he had planned this weekend. Without looking up, but smiling, he said, "I got a couple of cases of beer in the fridge. My old lady is away. I just got a couple of new porn movies in the mail. This one girl I used to fuck called me earlier today. She wants to come over. That's about it, guys." Because his head was down, the chief was unaware that there was a crowd of about five or six female petty officers standing not ten feet from him. They were all in shock from our exchange, but this actually made him seem more likeable from my perspective.

"You men have a great Navy weekend," said the chief as he walked outside. It was clear to Dan and me that the chief had our backs. He saluted, and we returned in kind.

When Bilzerian was done standing watch later that day, I stopped by his room. He was reading a paintball gun magazine when he opened his door. After he opened the door, he laid down on his rack. Back then, I could see his personality struggling to form. He spoke a mixed dialect of

Lethal Weapon, *Young Guns*, *Universal Soldier*, and *Point Break*. I was fluent in movie quotes, so there was no language barrier. Five years earlier, I was the 18-year-old who swung way too hard at every pitch. He was five years younger, so I had to repeat and explain my references more than I was used to.

"Do you ever go paintballing?" he asked.

"I've been a few times. The last one was when about a dozen of my fraternity brothers and I went to play. Some of us took shrooms before we went. It got out of hand when some of the regulars used frozen ammo against us. Being on mushrooms, it hurt in a different way. Several of my brothers and I got into fights on the course. That was about four years ago."

Dan handed me the magazine as he got up from his rack. He walked over to his desk, picked up an issue of *Robb Report*, and then resumed a supine position on his rack. Bilzerian looked like a little kid who dressed himself for the first time.

"Do you always dress like you're twelve? I get the whole comfort thing, but come on, dude. You're wearing Birkenstocks, a puffy rapper jacket, and bun hugger running shorts. You're dressed like a walking identity crisis Bilzerian!"

He did not make eye contact or respond to that comment. He got my point because that puffy jacket didn't make it out of Great Lakes.

"I was really into paintballing and built my own gun. It cost about $15,000 with all the aftermarket parts," he popped off without answering for his wardrobe.

"You a drug dealer? That's a lot of money for a toy gun."

"My paintball gun is no toy. I don't sell drugs. My dad's very wealthy."

"How wealthy?"

"His holding company owned Lockheed Martin. Here, take a look at this. My old man had this one. Each engine costs two million, and it's got four. He did the math on all the expenses associated with owning it. Everything including his two pilots was $30,000 and change just to get it in the air each time."

He proudly handed me the issue of *Robb Report* he was thumbing through. His finger was on the picture of his father's jet. I had bought issues of *Robb Report* at the bookstore at USC from time to time. It was something that I would flip through and fantasize about. *Robb Report* helped me nurture those pipe dreams of one day being able to afford one of the exotic cars that it often showcased. This issue had been extensively dog eared, highlighted, and underlined. For

Bilzerian, it seemed to be where he would brainstorm for his Christmas list. It was like a *Sharper Image* catalog for him.

"I had no idea that you could spend that much money on a paintball gun. That qualifies as 'Fuck you' money, I'd say."

"And I'm not even done with it yet. You should see my assault rifles at home. They're all tricked out."

"I like guns but don't have any. My father and I used to shoot trap a bunch."

I have bad ADHD. Dan's is worse. There were little or no segues when we spoke.

"Nice. Howard, you ever done a cycle?"

"I've been on two runs. Deca by itself for six weeks. I also stacked Anadrol, Halotestin, and Parabolan for eight weeks."

"What did it do to you?"

"Jesus, man. They're a felt experience. Ridiculous strength, size, and recovery on both cycles. I didn't use hero-sized doses of anything because I didn't need to. A few of my fraternity brothers ran the same gear in the same amounts for the same durations. They all made considerable gains as well."

"It says here that if you use enough Parabolan you'll piss blood. That stuff sounds awesome, but very toxic. What did it do to you?"

"I read that about a year ago. It's five times stronger than testosterone, so it's probably five times as toxic. Well, I never peed any blood. At my peak, I could do sets of chess press on a Hammer Strength with 680 pounds. I had spider veins galore. That stack turned my head into a GG Allin and the Murder Junkies concert. All I wanted to do was kill and fuck everything in my path. I had three girls who were up for anything anytime. It didn't matter. I was always angry."

"Hey, Howard. I was going to the gym in a bit. Do you want to work out?"

"Does Howdy Doody have wooden nuts?"

"Who the fuck's Howdy Doody?"

"Are you for real? You look just like the fucking guy and you've never heard of him?"

"I'm ready to rock Angelo! Where do you want me?" Dan popped off with that line from *Point Break*.

"Very good Dan. Welcome to Sea World, kid." If he wanted to speak in movie lines, let it be. Young men in our situation seemed to speak almost exclusively in obscure action movie quotes.

"Let's do a swim after and then grab dinner."

I went back to my room and grabbed my workout gear. The weather was getting colder almost every day now that we were into October. I was out front for only about a minute or two before Bilzerian came across the quarterdeck.

21

It was less than a half-mile from our barracks to the gym, so a sweatshirt was enough. We got there, showed our ID's, and got to it.

"Why don't we do some pushups and pull-ups to warm up, Howard?" he suggested as we approached a pull-up bar.

"Care to do some half-count jumping jacks also?" I laughed at him. We went back and forth between the two for about fifteen minutes. "Let's do upper body."

"I'm down. Wanna max out on anything?" he inquired insistently.

"Do what you want, but I'm not doing less than eight reps of anything. We're swimming afterwards."

"How else will we know who's stronger?" he said sideways.

"I know. I have at least twenty-five pounds and five years on you."

That upset him when I said it. It did not stop him from competing with me on every exercise. On every movement, I was at least proportionally stronger than Dan. About ninety minutes after we arrived, I asked him if he was ready for a swim.

"Alright, let's go to the pool," he mumbled, sounding half defeated. "How about we do a run after dinner?"

"Why not?"

We arrived at the pool and wasted no time grabbing two open lanes. We did four 500-yard sets of breast and combat side stroke, all of which I won.

"You might have won, but that's because you were doing more breaststroke than I was. When we get to Basic Underwater Demolition school (BUDs), I heard that you only really do combat side stroke because you're in fins the whole time."

He felt compelled to mention every potential factor which may have helped me outperform him in each instance. It became very apparent after that first workout together just how insecure Bilzerian was. He was noticeably upset every time I beat him at something. It seemed physically uncomfortable, or even a little painful for him, to compliment me when I outperformed him. I had a few training partners who were older and more intense. All that ever did was make me want me to train up to another level. Dan wasn't satisfied with finishing second.

"I'll sleep better knowing that, Dan. What's your point?"

"I was just saying that I could've beat you if we did the same stroke."

"I wouldn't be so sure. Besides, I'm not going to BUDs. I'm going to Special Warfare Combat Crewman (SWCC)."

"What the shit? Why SWCC?"

"Got sick in Basic. I contracted cellulitis."

"What's that?" he asked.

"It's an infection that attacks the joints. They swell up and get filled with fluid. My drill instructor (RDC) wouldn't let me go to medical right away. It was getting worse by the day, and she ignored my requests for medical attention. One day during week three, I woke up and couldn't stand or walk. My ankles were purple and like softballs. As I crawled to the head, someone got the chief. She asked me what was wrong. I unloaded on her while she called for help. Two barracks petty officers carried me to medical. I was rushed into the building and seen immediately. The doctor told me that I was within two days from being a double amputee. I was given a ton of meds and put on bed rest for almost two weeks. They could have sent me home. When I came off bed rest, it felt like my legs had atrophied to almost nothing. I started to go to the Dive Motivator workouts, but I hadn't passed the screen test for BUDs yet. All my scores were great, but I couldn't pass the run to save my life. My lower legs just had no kick or power. After I failed for the third time, they said that I had one more chance to pass. Otherwise, I was headed to the fleet."

"That fucking sucks," he interjected.

"On my last try, I swallowed my ego and screened for SWCC and passed. Spending two years with a Special Boat Unit easily beats the shit out of going undesignated to the fleet for two years."

"That makes perfect sense. My detailer is going to send me to the fleet if my stress fractures don't heal up soon. I'd rather go to BUDs broken and take my chances. Do you want to race 100 yards each stroke?"

"Do you mean a 400-yard Individual Medley, or race each stroke separately?"

"I meant each stroke by itself," he insisted.

"Pussy. Sure." I laughed.

I let him start us on each race. He was close with me for the breaststroke. On the other three, I pulled a little further away. He did not seem satisfied that I had beat him in all strokes. It would not let go of him. He challenged me to some sort of free weight medley and swim contest. He was desperate for a win on his record.

"The incline dumbbell fly and 500 yd. sidestroke is not an event. Let it go. We'll find something that you are better at soon enough. Let's eat before the galley gets crowded. Run later."

We showered, changed, and hustled over to the galley for dinner. Bilzerian had great abs back then and he ate that way. He certainly flexed them enough. He had the same build as now but weighed about 165. I ate like an offensive lineman and had the corresponding mid-section to show. I had almost thirty pounds on Bilzerian then. More than half of that was fat.

"How will we know where's one and a half miles?" I grilled him lightly.

"There's a course marked off on the street. You run a lap around part of the base and finish just down the street from the barracks."

"Easy enough. Why don't we meet up in front of the barracks in one hour stretched and ready? You got a watch?"

"Yep, I got a watch."

We were just running a mile and a half for time in sneakers. No boots, dungarees, or screen test. Wearing a ring watch, he showed up around a minute after me. Neither of us wasted any time. We were both ready to go. He looked at me, then at his ring.

"Ready, set, go."

We were off. Bilzerian started out ahead by just a little. He extended that lead to no less than 200 yards when he finished. It was no surprise that he beat me that cleanly. I had my work cut out for me. It had been a little less than three months since I got cellulitis. My time was almost a minute slower than before.

"How would Instructor Duel train around stress fractures?" I asked Bilzerian about a minute after finishing.

"I think he'd just drink more the night before. That guy's a machine. He used to come straight from the bar stool to base. He ran morning PT all the time. That guy worked us into the ground just working off his hangover."

Instructor Duel was one of the Dive Motivators at Great Lakes. He stood out against the other SEALs in that office for a few reasons. The guy never wore a uniform. He was almost always hungover but was in ridiculous shape. Pre 9/11, he was one of the more decorated SEALs, and he'd been on something like fifteen back-to-back deployments. He was a Navy Cross recipient. Viggo Mortensen looked like his clone in *GI Jane*, but only his mustache and hair were not as non-regulation as Duel's. Apparently, he broke his ankle falling off the high rope on the O Course at BUDs. That meant he probably spent over a year at that place which is twice as long as a normal stay. That meant his steel was folded more times than most. You could see it in his eyes. It made you want to look at his forehead or chest. He didn't look at people, he looked right through them.

"Do your lower legs hurt when you run? Mine don't. I just feel like I don't have any real leg drive."

Losing to him did not bug me in the least. It was not being able to move the way I was accustomed to which drove me more than half crazy. We called it quits after that run. I swear that if I had won, Bilzerian would have wanted to go best of three. As we walked back to the barracks, we saw a bunch of sailors acting like one beer queers in front of the club on base. We wanted nothing to do with any of them as we walked past them and into the barracks for the night.

There was an incredibly pedestrian social scene at Great Lakes. It had nothing to offer that I had not already done as a pre-teen. Not that I was antisocial, I simply was used to a much more intense scene. On all sides, I was surrounded by a bunch of teenagers who had never been away from home. Most of these kids had never even finished a four pack of wine coolers before.

The social scene that I was in the four years prior out in Los Angeles had a body count. It was packed to the hilt with meaningful pursuits like dealing cocaine to unscrupulous FBI agents, starring in porno movies, being ridiculously high on drugs and blackout drunk for four years straight, occasionally overdosing on drugs, tons of casual and unprotected sex, fighting a lot, and stealing everything that wasn't nailed down. I left some awesomely deep, albeit damaging, footprints between Hollywood and Newport Beach.

At Great Lakes, those of us who were going to special programs were basically targets in a reverse racism and sexism shooting gallery. Half the guys I met and knew who were going to BUDs never made it because of some bullshit violation. Guys would get popped for underage drinking, sexual harassment (whether real or imagined), possession of a fake I.D., or whatever the barrack's chief or leading petty officer could dig up on a guy. I have never seen people so jealous of things they did not want any part of. Fleet sailors hated us simply because they thought we got special treatment in special programs. That is true. It was not the kind of special treatment any sane person would ask for. Within the first week, some chief asked me if I had been approved to shave my head.

"Those with receding hairlines are permitted to do so under Navy regulations, Chief. I was told this by the duty officer at the barracks just the other day," I popped off. Big mistake.

"Are you telling me my business, seaman?" he screamed at me as he closed the distance between us and violated my personal space.

"You must be a wannabe SEAL. How would you like to go to the fleet instead, punk?" The Bates Lites boots, the twenty-inch neck, and the shaved head screamed "special programs" to Fleet non-commissioned officers. He meant it. I said nothing further.

Little conflicts like that popped up every few days while I was stationed there. When female sailors accused their male counterparts of anything, that was the end of it. All a guy had to be was accused of something and his dreams of special programs were over. There were a few females on base who could rub shoulders with the girls I was accustomed to at the University of Southern California. It was no surprise their dance cards were always full. They were constantly catered to by crowds of sailors, and I did not feel like waiting my turn. The rest had Navy issued asses and did not make the cut, so I never even bothered. I was not about to lose my orders over an angry pussy hunt gone wrong.

The Gurnee Mills Mall was the closest movie theatre to base. Located in Kenosha, WI, it was about a forty-minute shuttle van ride to Great Lakes. Time passed very slowly, especially on the weekends. It moved slow enough that we would arrive to movies on time and even a few minutes early. That meant there was a half hour before the previews started. One time before *The Sixth Sense* came on, there was a trivia contest. I cleaned house and got every question correct. The final question was for a bunch of free movie passes. "What movie featured Tom Hanks and Bruce Willis?" I was the only one there who knew the answer: *Bonfire of the Vanities.* Dan and I saw *Stigmata, The World is Not Enough,* and

American Beauty with the passes. That was how we chewed up the remainder of Saturdays and Sundays after we'd finished training.

There were a few decent eateries at Gurnee, with Rainforest Café being my favorite. The restaurant was set up to look like the Amazon Rainforest. They even had exotic animals and birds. Dan and I ate there often. The food was great, as was the service. There were two gorgeous waitresses working there at the time.

"Howard, did you have a contract coming in?" Dan fired politely at me while sitting at the bar.

"Did! But don't now..." I said without looking up from my dinner.

"What the shit do you mean?"

"I did have a contract, but I lost it. Three weeks before I left, I got in a high-speed chase and got twelve tickets. It was reduced, but that voided my contract. I came in anyways. It was part of my rehabilitation."

Speaking with his mouth overstuffed, like usual, Dan interrupted, "What do you mean part of your rehabilitation? Do you mind telling me about the chase?"

"What do you want to know?"

"Everything. Tell me the whole story?"

"Alright. I'd been out all night partying with good friends in Albany, NY. At about 1:30 AM I drove my friend

Bill and his girlfriend Gabby home with like thirty drinks in me."

"When Bill got out of the car, he looked at me. He said over the music, 'You have one left and two right turns to get to your parents. It's one mile. Go home.'"

He walked into his parents' house with Gabby.

"I turned right and went back downtown to another bar, the Plaza Grill. I knew that I had two girls who would play me in Canadian doubles. Not only was this a no-brainer, this was a no-looker. I did the math in my head.

"Earlier in the day I had knocked the rearview mirror off my windshield. I was coaching lacrosse at the time. I'd caught my long pole, which is six feet, on the mirror when I took it out after practice earlier that day. Unaware of what was behind me, I was doing well over 100 miles an hour before I got into downtown Albany. That Stone Temple Pilots song, 'Where the River Goes,' was blaring so loud, I can still hear it. I ran at least a dozen intersections as I made it to State Street at about 80 miles an hour. I cranked the wheel to the left and pulled the parking brake. That induced a 180-degree brake slide into a perfectly executed parking job in between two cars. That move was of divine inspiration. Until then, I had been ignorant to what was happening in the wake behind me. I looked down at the stereo to turn it off and take the face off the Alpine. As I reached to put it in the glove box, I looked up and I could see no less than seven cop cars. I instantly sobered up enough to realize that there was no way that I was going to be able to talk my way out of this. I had no idea that any cops were after me, let alone seven cruisers. I took my keys and threw them up onto the roof of my car. I kept both of my hands out of the window and clearly visible until the officers were next to the car. One opened the door and two others helped me out of the vehicle. I may have been tougher than any one of the police officers individually, but I was not tougher than all ten of them at the same time. I did not act otherwise. When they cuffed me, I didn't resist. I was repeatedly asked to submit to a field sobriety test and take a breathalyzer. 'I have a sprained ankle so no monkey tricks. Take me to the hospital and take a blood sample. I refuse the breathalyzer!' I said."

Back then you could still refuse the breathalyzer and the penalties weren't worse than a DUAI like it is now. Your license was not automatically suspended, and it didn't cost you $13,000 minimum. Refusing the breathalyzer angered the officers.

"'I'm giving you one more chance,' one of them said."

"'Shove that chance up your fucking ass and take me to jail,' I cut him off."

"They never did find the roach that was in the ashtray. All they had to do was look. I wound up with twelve tickets from the stop and spent the night in jail. I puked while being booked. Eventually, I got put into a holding cell with the rest of the evening's all-stars. I was dressed to the nines and some punk stood up and made some sort of pointing gesture to me. I stepped in with a straight left to his cheek and knocked him back against the wall. I can't confirm what happened after because the next thing I remembered was waking up alone in a cell with a bad hangover and stiff neck. My asshole wasn't sore, so I felt optimistic.

"At the arraignment, the next morning I was the only person released on his own recognizance. There were guys there for attempted murder, rape, and assault. Drunk driving, resisting arrest, public intoxication, reckless endangerment, reckless driving, unreasonable and imprudent speed, and failure to yield to traffic symbols were minor fractures of the law comparatively."

"About two weeks later, I had to go to court. My father is a prominent attorney. Twelve tickets got reduced to two. I got two points on my license, a $500 fine, and a six-month suspension. I could have had that upgraded to a conditional license, but I would be at Basic in two weeks. One of my father's partners was close with the DA. He told me not to speak at all in court. When the judge called my case, someone handed him a sheet of paper and whispered something in his ear for about ten seconds. His facial expression changed as he eyeballed me. My attorney whispered in my ear that we were to approach the bench. He reminded me not to speak."

"'Joel's son or not, if I ever find you in my court again, I will throw the fucking book at you!' the Judge muttered under his breath."

The five-year-old in me wanted to start giggling when he swore, but the 23-year-old barely knew better.

"When a person gets a DUAI or DUI, there's basically a curriculum one must complete to eventually get the charges dropped and gain one's license back. That course load can last several months. My lawyer said to the judge that getting me on my way to Basic Training was the most beneficial solution for all parties. I can only imagine the trouble I would have gotten into while going to drivers' impact awareness classes for six months living at home. And that, Bilzerian, is how I lost my contract."

"That's wild. I got into some trouble of my own. I was living with my parents near Salt Lake City, Utah and going to school there. A couple of my friends had a run-in with some of the guys on the football team. We were outnumbered, and I didn't want to get jumped. So I grabbed my assault rifle in the back of my car. Somebody called the cops on me. I was detained and my car was searched. The police found my assault rifle and arrested me."

I'm not a gun nut, so most of what he described regarding the aftermarket parts of his weapon and upgrades was lost in translation. Nothing on it was stock. When he mentioned how the ammunition was stacked in his magazines, I paid attention.

"I staggered them tracer, armor piercing, hollow point," he was glowing with pride over this. "The cops wanted to nail me to the wall for just the ammo."

I looked at him in a way that a child would look at a museum exhibit. "Hate to be the voice of reason here, Dan. When a high school kid is found in possession of a greatly modified assault rifle, loaded with tactical ammunition, that's going to do more than raise a few eyebrows. They probably thought your nickname was Slick and your file was three feet thick. For all they knew you were one of the guys who escaped from the North Hollywood bank robbery a few years back. I'm not judging you, just exercising some objectivity. Did your father kick your ass when he found out? Also, why didn't you just fight your way out? Pulling a gun is kind of a bitch move."

That last question may as well have been in Sumerian. I could easily tell that Dan was averse to getting into physical conflicts. He was more afraid of being punched in the face than he was of dying. We're all terrified of something.

"I spent a few days in jail before they called my family. My dad didn't really flip out. I could tell he was disappointed without him yelling. He was more upset that I refused to call him."

I could tell then that all Dan ever wanted to be was like his dad. I wondered if Paul Bilzerian knew how hardcore he was. It's my opinion that Paul has never given it a thought. He's too busy winning his way. It's a good way to be, but a hard line to tow.

"Man, have I been there. My dad gave me a world class guilt trip when he found out that I had been expelled from college and kept it from him for a year."

"It took your family over a year to find out that you were expelled? What the fuck? You've got to be kidding. How'd you get away with that?"

"Dan, it doesn't matter how it may seem. Nobody ever gets away with anything. Don't change the subject. What happened to your legal issues?"

"My father was in the Army. One of his friends from back then is a two-star general now. He had it expunged from my record. I was banned from the state of Utah for over a year. Otherwise, it went away. I got my GED instead of going back to school."

"It sounds like that major general owed your dad a favor. What did your dad do in the army?"

"He was one of the youngest commissioned Green Berets in Vietnam. My old man was legit. He even had the Special Forces pushup record at one point. When he got out, he went to Stanford, and then Harvard Business School. He was a high school dropout before that."

It was now even more apparent that he was very fond of his father and the path he blazed through life.

"Sounds like an interesting guy."

"He's owned and ran a couple of companies since. When we lived in Tampa, he was the CEO of a holding company. He had an NBA regulation court and scoreboard built in the basement. My dad used to have mandatory 6:00 AM workouts for his Executive Vice Presidents every morning. He'd wear a referee jersey and he had a platinum whistle. They were doing three-man weaves and scrimmaging under his tutelage for like 90 minutes on weekdays."

I did not have to be a clinical psychologist to understand why Dan wanted to be a SEAL. He wanted to follow in his father's footsteps. Making it through the program would have erased his past transgressions. I was after the same marker. Graduating BUDs would have more than offset my four year, XXX-rated, felony-filled spring break at USC. We had a common denominator which is one of the main reasons we clicked. We were both over-privileged discipline cases who were playing catch-up.

I stood up from the bar where we sat and walked over to where one of the waitresses was handling an alligator. Both creatures interested me at that moment. After a minute or so, both seemed highly impractical at the time. The devil on my left shoulder wanted both of them more than the angel on my right shoulder. Doing the math in my head there, however, it was determined that I wouldn't ask for her phone number. Even though she was appealing in every manner to my senses, what were the chances? What were the chances we would hit it off like a gas fire and I would move her out with me? What were the chances that this one was going to be my future ex-wife? What would it take for me to willingly reside in Kenosha? How big would the gator have to be for it to kill me in my sleep? All answered in a blink of an eye. I walked back over to Bilzerian at the bar. My margarita was half empty before I reached for it. We paid the check and hopped a shuttle van back to base.

"Hey Howard, what two tickets did you end up getting?"

Other than the driver, there was nobody in the van except Dan and me. "Refusal to submit to a chemical test, and failure to yield to a traffic signal. My recruiter wrote it up improperly, and I was two days from going to the Fleet undesignated until I had the file in hand to show Chief Nagle."

"Parents do anything?"

"My father didn't flinch. He just said that he assumed I wanted help with it. I said, 'Yes, please,' and that was that. He never mentioned it again. My old man was a knuckle-dragging wild man before I was. He was known to fight three people at once. He also wrecked three Corvettes while driving drunk at the same age I am now."

We were headed to Gurnee Mills in an empty shuttle van the next day. Earlier we switched it up and swam first before the gym. Dan remembered something from the other night.

"Hey Howard, how did you keep your parents in the dark about being expelled for over a year?"

"Pure fucking talent, Howdy Doody, pure talent."

"Ha ha. Seriously, how'd you get away with it?"

"I didn't get away with anything. I got way ahead of some things for a few years. It was a legendary run by any standard. My first real power move came when I changed my mailing address from my parents' house in Albany to my fraternity house in Los Angeles during my second semester. This allowed me to screen all written correspondence between USC and my parents. That, along with some creative storytelling, bought me over a year of burning it from both ends with impunity. At the start of my third semester in the fall of '95, the house had me down as suspended from Kappa Sigma National for fighting. That didn't mean shit in our house. I was a phantom, bro. I wasn't on any grade list. That kept me from lowering the house GPA. When spring '96 rolled around I had to keep it going."

"Keep what going?" he inquired.

"The ultimate ride. *Point Break* style, bitch. I opted for the tuition insurance when I enrolled after my first semester. In spring '96, I made it work for me. I traded two eight balls of coke for a legit doctor's note. It was from a general practitioner out in the Valley. He wrote that I tested positive for mono. I was put on bed rest for eight weeks, given plenty of codeine syrup and hydrocodone. This also meant that the tuition bill would be refunded. I went to the Bursar's Office and tried to get a check cut to me. They said that it'd be refunded to my father's credit card. A poorly explained refund would cause as many problems as it would fix. My next stop was to the Office of Degree Progress. There, I purchased two pages of blank stationary for $100 from a secretary I followed out of the building on a smoke break. I forged a letter on it to my parents. It said that I had won a scholarship from my fraternity for having the most improved GPA in the chapter. It stated that my next semester would be tuition free. I still can't believe that they bought it.

There's more still. A year later, I convinced my parents that I was going to spend a semester at Santa Monica City College and take acting classes in Hollywood. That went over without any pushback. It wasn't until Christmas 1997 that I gave up the act. Nine semesters between USC and Santa Monica City College and only two classes completed."

We were back on base before I was done with story time.

A few days later we were watching *Caddyshack* in Bilzerian's room after swimming. "Howard, were you around when Burley got caught at the airport?"

"He was a little ahead of me. I do remember, though. I was in the waiting room at the Dive Motivators Office when they all returned from his captain's mast. I saw Duel in a dress uniform that one time. He had more medals and ribbons than any five admirals could wear. I have never seen a more decorated uniform in person."

There was this special program guy Burley who went through Basic right around when Bilzerian and I did. During his A School at Great Lakes, he was in Chicago O'Hare Airport set to go home on leave. He had bought a Trident and Navy Cross at the PX on base. He then wore both on his uniform and was stopped by someone who doubted his medal stack. After being cross examined, Burley said that he was with DEVGRU and had been doing black counter-drug ops with Duel in South America. After his altercation with Burley, the doubter contacted the Dive Motivator's Office and Burley was put on restriction and blackballed for life. He was in the process of getting kicked out for stolen valor. I heard that he was ordering Finaplix pellets and making bathtub Trenbolone to pass the time before his discharge. All the SEALs from the Dive Motivator's Office went to see Burley get spit roasted. I bet Duel was pissed he had to get in uniform. We could go on about him for days.

It takes one to know one. Of the thousands of sailors stationed at Great Lakes when I was, there were maybe 50 guys slotted for special programs. I could look at a guy and know he was headed to special programs. It would be like this test. Take a medium sized college campus and make it completely fragrance free. Then give every 200th person a hero's dose of Drakkar Noir. You could tell who was wearing it with the same margin of error. The first time that I met my future late roommate Edward Austin Koth, I just knew. We wound up being in Class 234 together, but he did not wear Drakkar.

There is clearly something embedded in the hard wiring of those types drawn to those jobs. We carried ourselves a certain way. A few weeks before Bilzerian and I left Great Lakes, we met Fennel, another BUDs guy. He had just moved in a few hours earlier when he passed me in the hall and politely asked me if I had a chew for him. He said he had been to BUDs and got dropped in Third Phase. He was from Texas and had the eyes of a crazy person like the chief. He was at Great Lakes for A School as well, then headed back to his ship in San Diego, then hopefully back to BUDs. He said that he had made it to Third Phase but sprained his ankle. Then he washed out because he failed a timed run or two while on San Clemente Island. He was married and had off-base housing when he was there. His marriage had already gone to shit before BUDs started. He came home one day after training and one of his instructor friends was in bed with his wife. It didn't hit him right away as he walked to the kitchen and grabbed a beer. While he sat on his sofa drinking, his instructor came out of the bedroom and grabbed a beer as well. Then he said to him, "I guess I'll see you tomorrow then." A few days later when Fennel was running the O course, it hit him. That was one of hundreds of throwaway stories that I heard in the pipeline to and at BUDs.

Somehow the topic changed to training and then supplements. He said his "nutritionist" had him on both Hydroxycut and Xenadrine at the same time. She had upped his dose of both. Both had large amounts of caffeine and ephedra. The ingredient labels were almost identical. Back then both of those products alone felt like the Yellow Jackets that you could buy at a truck service station. Cheap speed. Anyway, that just always struck me funny that a "nutritionist" would make a recommendation like that. I should mention that he did not look lean at all. His drug of choice at BUDs was Winstrol. He indicated that one shot a week lowered his run time by about 2 minutes. That was something I wanted to believe. I never saw him again after I left Great Lakes. One of my friends back home had an interesting experience on Winstrol. It made him so agitated that he compulsively chewed his fingernails down to stumps. When he could no longer chew them, he took needle nosed pliers and pulled the rest of them off. I saw him at the mall right after he did so and asked him what had happened. That was one of those things I had to see with my own eyes to believe.

2

MILLINGTON, TENNESSEE
DECEMBER 1999

About a week before Christmas, we both left Great Lakes for our next duty stations. Dan was headed out to the Naval Special Warfare Center (NSWC) in Coronado, CA. I was headed down to Millington, TN. It was easy to fly below the radar there. This was the home of the aviation A Schools that are now in Pensacola, Florida. This was also where the Bureau of Personnel (BUPERS) was located. That was where all the orders for everyone in the Navy were cut. There were SEALs and other special programs guys shackled to desks for mandatory shore duty. Many of those guys were not meant for shore duty. There was a legendary master chief there at the same time I was. He drank thirty beers every night of the week without ever letting up. He was also at PT every morning burning them off at 5:00 AM. Guys like him should be perpetually deployed. It was my temporary duty station until getting a class slot at SWCC. Chris Kyle and a bunch of other guys were down there for the same reason. We were just staying sharp and waiting our turns. Life down there was much better than Great Lakes. It was at the end of my second week there when I developed stress fractures.

PT that Friday morning was a twelve-mile run. The senior chief told me that I was not expected to do the whole run. He suggested half. I did the whole thing. I felt depleted during the run. I was in the shower after and realized something was wrong. When the hot water hit my neck, I began to urinate. I looked down to see a black stream running down my leg. It turned red at the bottom of the bathtub. My lower legs were on fire at this point. I spent the rest of that morning icing my legs and drinking two gallons of water. The first of which went down in less than ten minutes. After PT on Monday morning the senior chief called me aside.

"Howard, drop. Why are you going SWCC and not BUDs?" he asked eyeballing me.

I dropped into the leaning rest and pushed out twenty push-ups.

"I got sick at Great Lakes and couldn't pass the test in boots after getting off bed rest. It wasn't my first choice, but I'd rather be with a Special Boat Unit for two years than the fleet, Senior," I answered while still in leaning rest.

"Would you still rather go to BUDs?'

"Yes, I would Senior."

"Recover. OK, then. You know that you shouldn't have run the whole course on Friday. You can get stress fractures running too much too soon."

I snapped up to attention.

"Yes, Senior."

"I'll have your orders changed this week."

"Thank you, Senior. What about the test?" he just smiled at me and said nothing.

"May I have permission to go to medical, Senior?"

"Sure. Why?"

"I may have gotten stress fractures on Friday."

"It wouldn't surprise me. Look, Howard, I can tell you have a hardcore mentality. That's why I am switching your program. You must temper that mindset with sound judgement. If you do have stress fractures, you're in a good place for them to heal. Now drop."

I hit the deck and sounded off another twenty push-ups. What a small price for such a huge favor.

"Recover, Howard. Go see about your legs."

It was a day or so before I was able to see Dr. Van Raden. She explained that she could order a nuclear bone scan, but it would be at least two weeks. Then, she suggested a more direct and conclusive test. She asked that I pull my pant legs up above my knees. I looked down at her hand, and in it was a tuning fork. She struck it on the end of the examination table where I sat. Then she proceeded to rub it up the inside of my right lower leg. It had not travelled six inches before I winced and groaned uncontrollably in agony. On the left leg, it was a little higher up and even more painful.

That sensation was on the same level as the metal Q-Tip STD Test which I know all too well. That level of pain often causes loss of consciousness for those who are unfamiliar.

"That was easy, see? Howard, you do in fact have bilateral stress fractures. I'm recommending you take it as easy as you can. Here's a chit for light and limited duty. Let's give it four months and we'll reevaluate." She had clearly done this before.

It had been a couple of weeks since I spoke with Dan. He'd made it out to Coronado, stress fractures and all. Early on, he pissed off his class's leading petty officer for some reason. Because of that, much of his class did not like him very much. The night before Hell Week, he rented a room at the Hotel Del Coronado and stayed there. He said that the water was about 55 degrees going into Hell Week with Class 229. He made it through. Nice.

Dan told me at one point that he had bought a supercharged Mustang Cobra on a lark and then three days later decided he didn't want the car anymore. He tasked Lance, the Bilzerian Family bodyguard, with the vehicle's return. Dan assured me that Lance was an expert at such matters. He would wear his revolver in his waistband and wear a few extra gold chains that day. Like clockwork, Lance picked up the Mustang from Dan and the dealer granted him a refund.

Dan also mentioned that he reconnected with Fennel. He was stationed in San Diego. Unfortunately, he had failed the screen test for BUDs and got stationed on a ship. There, he failed the screen test for Search and Rescue Swimmer (SAR) and was just a regular fleet sailor now.

Dan had already made his way south of the border to Tijuana and was seeing a physician once a week for a 4 mL dose of Laurabolan. That stuff is the Dane Cook of anabolic steroids. Weak ass stuff. Fennel had bought 1,000 tablets of Dianabol for about 50 bucks and had been on them for a long time. 50 mg a day for six months more than qualified him as a frustrated user. One time when they went down to Mexico to get drugs, they decided to get a couple of prostitutes. The one that Fennel hired would not blow him or fuck him without a condom. This became problematic because he could not get an erection with a condom on. Hypogonadism had set in, and this aggravated him. Apparently, he slapped his hooker and kicked her out of the room. He then went and bought two more pre-loads of testosterone, shot up, and went to go get another hooker, only to have the same result. One night at a dance club in San Diego, Fennel met Joey Lauren Adams. He acted as if he didn't know who she was, and the affair started then and there. It lasted a few months. His ship was set to go on deployment. He went AWOL with her for a couple of months until their relationship fizzled out. That was the last I ever heard about Fennel from Bilzerian.

Dan made it through Hell Week but got dropped from training at the end of first phase. According to him, he failed a timed run. He said the stress fractures were unbearable. Although, he never went to medical until after failing the run. He said that his lower legs were so bad that if they got any worse, they'd have to be surgically broken and then reset. I had no reason to doubt his word at the time. Future events would change that irreparably.

3

ALBANY, NEW YORK
MAY 2000

For about ten weeks, going from the beginning of May to the end of July, I was sent home from Tennessee on recruiting duty. That sounded like "double secret probation," whatever the hell that means. BUPERS found out that it had to pay a *per diem* to all special program candidates. They did everything they could to fuck us out of that money, but they wound up having to pay everyone stationed there $83 per day retroactively. Many of the officers above us tried telling us that we did not deserve the money and that we were burdening the command. It was easy to talk like that when they stayed in condos and dined at the Officer's Club. There was no dining facility on base for us because the galley had been closed. To this point, we were expected to feed ourselves properly on $8 per day. None of the rooms in the barracks had kitchens, not even microwaves. My buddy Worm used to let me use his George Foreman Grill. Three pounds of grilled chicken and steak per day did not get me as ripped as I thought. Drinking a twelve pack of Diet Sprite and double dosing on Xenadrine did not help further my cause. It was a feeble attempt at Keto, Motorhead style. In order to avoid paying us anymore than they had to already, they sent us all home on leave until our class spots opened up. I was paid around $9,000 right before I was sent home. A bunch of us went and got tattoos at Underground Ink in Memphis. Some of the EOD and Diver guys went out and got brand new trucks. Before leaving BUPERS, I made a few calls up to NY.

A few days after I arrived home, I acquired a respectable cycle of anabolics and androgens. I had dabbled in performance enhancing drugs before, but this was the first time that I applied some math to things. This was not to make my shirts fit tighter. This would be a major program upgrade. I grabbed Sostenon 250, Dianabol, Deca Durabolan, and plenty of Winstrol. The next two pages will either read like Sanskrit or Dr. Seuss depending on whether you are one of the initiated or not.

Sostenon 250 is a blend of four testosterone esters. It's an oil based injectable which becomes active within 24 hours and lasts a few weeks in the system. Because it is comprised of multiple esters in low doses, negative side effects associated with testosterone are held to a minimum. I used it only for the first five of ten weeks to get things going. Starting with 250 mg, ramping sharply up to 1,000 mg, and then off.

Dianabol was the only oral on the menu. Its effects can be felt within minutes. The half-life is about five hours.

I put all of the tabs in an Altoids container and took 10 mg every three hours. When using by itself, it is not uncommon to gain 30 pounds in the first month. I ramped up to 50 mg within a week. They say anything more than that is reserved for frustrated users, which I was not. Once at 50 mg, I cruised at that dose for four weeks and then tapered off over the next ten days.

Deca Durabolan is an exceptionally long and slow acting oil based injectable. If used alone, the effects may not be realized for up to a month. It helps the joints as well as recovery. I began with 200 mg per week for the first three. Then, I took it to 400 mg which is considered to be at the crossroads of safe and ideal for the next month. For the remainder, I dropped back to 200 mg and 100 mg per week for two weeks.

Winstrol rounded out the cocktail. It's a fast-acting water based injectable with a half-life of about 9 hours. Daily administration is what the cool kids do. This was the only drug I ran for the entire 10 weeks. I used 50 mg on normal days, and 100 mg on those days when I went above and beyond with my training. The muscle gains are not huge but basically permanent. I've been told by some elite track athletes that they would use it in the same syringe with cortisone and inject locally into an injury.

This little run took me from 191 lbs. up to 218 lbs. and then down to 184 lbs. My goal was not to get so big that I could not see my nipples without the help of a mirror. Healing my stress fractures, accelerated recovery, and not going catabolic during ridiculously intense and long workouts were the factors driving my choices.

When I got home, I bet against the market and never so much as even checked in with my recruiting office. There was no way that the people in BUPERS were going to reach out and contact our recruiters to see that we were being adequately babysat. I spent all of my time training and partying.

At one point I made an outing to Charlestown, MA to see my buddy Sniggiho. My childhood country club doubles tennis partner had been a Bostonian since he attended Boston College in the early 90's. On Friday night, we ate some ecstasy and went to Club Avalon. I found an off-duty stripper with a shiny one-piece dress to occupy a few of my senses. I lost track of her at closing time, which was at one o'clock. That was, and still is, one of my problems with Boston. One o'clock was too early to call it quits in a town that parties like that. We grabbed an eight ball of coke around two and finished it by mid-morning. That whole next day was spent in recovery mode on his sofa smoking weed and drinking Bloody Marys. We watched *Heat* and *Any*

Given Sunday. We hit the gym later, but it wasn't an "above and beyond" session.

We were out with two of his buddies from BC the night before. I met Brian all the way back in the beginning of my senior year in high school. I met Aaron on a similar outing about a year prior. After our performance on Friday, Saturday was a rebound night. The four of us and Aaron's girlfriend went out to dinner downtown. The ecstasy finally felt like it had worn off while we were at the table. Dinner went by without incident. What happened in the parking structure after dinner was a different story.

I rode home with Brian. Sniggiho, Aaron, and his girlfriend went in the other car. Brian backed out of the parking spot and put the car in drive. We pulled around a corner of this multi-level parking structure. Just then, I looked to my right and saw an SUV. The driver-side door was ajar, and the driver stood between the door and the frame of the car. He appeared to be holding it up. He was about to throw up. As I panned to my left, I saw a kid riding shotgun who appeared to be leaning down to snort a line of cocaine at that very moment. Jackpot! I told Brian to pull up and park in the next open parking space. I was out of the car before he even slowed down. I scurried over to those two guys in that SUV. Bingo. I was right. The driver had just puked and wiped his face as he turned to face me. The kid in shotgun was doing a rail of coke. A big one. This was a timed evolution. If I moved too slow the police may get wise. If I pushed too hard, I would scare these two NASCAR fans off before I accomplished the objective.

"You guys look like you could use a hand," I said calmly as I rapidly closed what little distance was between us.

"Huh?" they both said in unison.

The kid in shotgun looked up from the CD case in his lap. The driver turned to face me as he wiped some vomit from his face with his Dale Earnhardt shirt.

"You're in over your heads. You look like one or both of you are going to overdose before you finish that baggie. You look like you've been up for a week."

"Yeah. How the fuck did you know?'

"I'm just like you, but only on day two. I'm not a cop. Me and my friends were at it last night. When we just drove past you, I knew what was up. I could tell you needed help. I'm going to do you a favor. Here's $80. I'm taking what's left. That way you guys can call it quits," I instructed.

They were in no condition to put up a fight and they actually seemed relieved. I have been there too many times myself.

"Really? You're not a cop? Thanks bro," they each said as they shook my hand and smiled at me. The driver patted me on the shoulder.

"I'd get out of here, like *now*. Go home and sleep for a few days," I remarked as I turned and hustled over to my ride.

"Nice fucking job. Real smooth man. I saw the whole thing," Brian said smiling ear-to-ear.

"Those guys were in rough shape. It was the fraternal thing to do," I laughed but was serious. "Let's pull onto the roof and make this disappear."

We quickly dispensed with formalities and poured the two grams or so onto a CD case. We made it disappear in six rails. Neither of us spoke for the half hour that we drove home. I sat on Sniggiho's couch for like another two hours not talking, watching *The Man with the Golden Gun,* completely numb from the waist up.

4

SAN DIEGO, CALIFORNIA
AUGUST 2000

I had to fly down and check out of BUPERS in Millington before I went to Coronado. In early August of 2000, I finally arrived in Coronado. Class 232 Hell Week was underway when I arrived at the Naval Special Warfare Center. I was set to start in class 233. For the first few days, I stayed across the street from the NSWC at the Amphibious Base. The Amphibious Base was adjacent to the galley which was a mile away from the NSWC. At BUDs, students run to and from each meal. In a week of training, students will run forty-five miles just to eat.

I moved across the street before Hell Week was secured. Enough guys had dropped, so Building 618 had vacant rooms. Dan was doing shore duty now that his ship was back from Okinawa after being dropped from BUDS. He was a quartermaster and SAR while underway. Currently, he was working at the pass and decal office in San Diego. He stopped by the first weekend. By then, I'd been moved across the street to Building 618. He pulled up in his white Jeep Grand Cherokee. It had a better suspension, lift, and bigger tires than the Suburbans used on base as ambulances. This was a nice ride for a sailor making E-3 pay. We shook hands and traded insults in front of the temporary barracks where I was staying. Bilzerian looked at his watch about two minutes into our debriefing each other. He opened the back of his Jeep to mix a protein shake. He was all about eating every two hours like clockwork.

"Are you OK Dan?" I said sarcastically.

"I need to eat every two hours during the day," he mumbled with half a Nature's Valley Granola Bar stuffed in his mouth.

"Nature's Valley? Man, you're really slumming it like us real people now. What happened to the Boulder Bars?" I laughed. Boulder Bars were these organic high-end food bars that he seemed to have an endless supply of at Great Lakes.

"I ran out." He mixed a Myoplex in a red plastic cup. "Howard, in Rosarito they have pre-loaded syringes of Sostenon 250 for $11. How about a quick trip south?"

"Absolutely. Stop talking with your mouth full. Calm down and finish your Chihuahua piss smoothie first." That caused him to laugh and spit his shake all over the hind driver's side quarter panel.

"Fucking great! Howard, make sure the coast is clear." He pulled up the leg of his shorts and attempted to urinate the chocolate shake off his Jeep.

We hopped into the Jeep and headed for the main gate on base. All BUDs and SWCC students were strictly forbidden to enter Mexico. Bad things have happened to sailors down there. It was a disqualifying offense, but guys went all the time. The only way we would get into trouble was if we got caught. We agreed that we wouldn't allow ourselves to get caught. As we would have it, the same car in front of us when we left base was the same car that parked across from us when we arrived in Rosarito.

The team guy got out of his car and walked into the veterinary pharmacy. We waited a few minutes before we did the same. On the sidewalk, we passed this jacked guy wearing a "Got Fina?" t-shirt. That stopped Bilzerian and I both in our tracks. Fina was a cattle implant that through some chemical process had some form of Trenbolone available within it. The shirt was basically an insider joke which loosely translates to "Got juice?"

Inside that pharmacy was every performance enhancing substance known to man, horse, and dog. However, we really didn't want to risk smuggling illegal substances across the Mexican-US border. I got pinched in 1995 at the same border crossing with steroids.

The pharmacies right across the border are always under surveillance. Often, they'd even call ahead to the border patrol and customs agents to report *gringo* smugglers.

Usually, the pharmacy gets the seized merchandise back for free or for fire sale prices. It's a great little enterprise they have going. My buddy and I got detained and put in a holding cell. Some other guy who got popped for the same thing an hour earlier was in the cell. He said the customs agents talked about us for an hour before we got caught. They watched for a guy with sunglasses and a guy with a yellow button-down shirt. I wanted to go back to the pharmacy with a baseball bat and exact retribution, but my associate reasoned with me.

In the hours we waited to get charged and bailed out, we saw people get busted with all sorts of stuff. A 16-year-old Mexican kid got caught trying to enter America with a full stick of dynamite. They didn't charge him with anything and sent him back to Mexico. A woman got picked up in a pregnant costume with five keys of cocaine where the baby should have been. They didn't let her go free. My associate and I were both given Class C Felonies. It wouldn't be an issue unless we were caught again. I am still surprised that the incident never showed up during my top-secret, or better, background check that I had done to get orders to BUDs. We wanted to stock up but had no way of getting it over the border safely.

Bilzerian and I opted for the pre-loaded syringes of Sostenon 250. Sostenon 250 was made up of four different length testosterone esters. Two of them were long acting, so if we missed a week here and there, it didn't impact our hormone patterns much. We could inject them and dispose of them, which made crossing the border safer. We stopped at a gas station and took turns pinning in the stall in the restroom. Then, we went over to Señor Frog's for a few tacos. That first trip was a success, so weekly field trips became an occurrence for the next ten months or so.

We knew enough not to mess around down there any more than we had to. On one trip, Dan and I had to. Somewhere between the pharmacy and the beach, we were in an accident. Some guy on a bicycle rode right into us while we were stopped at a stop sign. The guy on the bike was not hurt, but terribly upset that he hit us. When he stood up, he belligerently screamed at us in the Jeep. Dan froze. I jumped out of the car and walked around the back to the other side. The elapsed time around the car was maybe two seconds. In those two seconds, I visualized many outcomes and consequences. We could get lynched by the locals. Second, we could wind up doing time in a Mexican prison. Getting robbed, kidnapped, or killed by the police was not a stretch either. I saw a straight line to freedom all the way to America. Without hesitation, I hit him on the left jawline from his eight o'clock. I swung just as he turned to face me. He was out cold before hitting the ground. One pedestrian then stepped towards the Jeep as if that was his friend. I made two or three steps to tighten up our geometry. I swung even harder at that guy. I tried to kill him with one punch. He did not go down as clean, but he didn't get up either. I hurt myself almost as much. A few days later when doing the Obstacle Course (O Course), my left serratus and back complex were still on fire because of that second target. I jumped back into Dan's Jeep, and we sped all the way up to the border and crossed over without incident or making a sound. In the two seconds between when I got out of Bilzerian's Jeep to when I engaged the first target, the sense of speed and accuracy overwhelmed me. The tremors of impact made my torso spasm so violently they almost made me vomit. That went on for an hour after we crossed the border. What happened was not our fault in the least. It was our responsibility to get back into America safely. I was not about to get raped or murdered or let Dan meet the same fate. That would certainly qualify as a "skydiving without a parachute moment."

There was one other trip down to Rosarito when we encountered some interference. We had done our thing and were just getting on to the highway to go north. About a mile into the return trip there were a few military vehicles that formed a roadblock. Soldiers pulled several vehicles to the side including us. We had nothing illegal in Dan's Jeep. It was unsettling as the soldiers pointed their assault rifles at us while others turned the Jeep upside down. The ordeal was over within an hour and we were free to go.

I had an adverse experience in Cabo San Lucas on Spring Break in 1995 that helped shape my decision-making process. What happened to me down there was so fucked up that I vowed to never be in a situation like that again.

To give perspective, the Macarena was a top ten song during that week down there. Joe Francis, owner of Girls Gone Wild started his empire on that Spring Break that week. He was at USC when I was there. 4,000 students were in Cabo that week. Only five of them got arrested. Four of us were in the same suite. We had grain alcohol on the flight down. Four of us finished a case of *cervezas* from the airport to the Hotel Plaza Las Glorias. Upon arrival we jumped into the pool with clothes on and sat at the pool bar for margaritas. Fifteen minutes later we made it up to the suite where we polished off an eight ball of cocaine. One of my brothers brought it down in his sock and said nothing until we were in the suite. Things escalated sharply into bar fights, coeds, prostitutes, vandalism, and pick pocketing. Two of our crew went missing after the second night. We finally checked the jail and there they were. We bailed them out and the *Federales* locked them up again. It got so bad that we had to contact the Embassy for help. On the last day they showed up at our suite again with Uzis demanding they lock up Andy and Raj again. I tried to get the rest of my brothers to back me up and jump them when they were not expecting it. One of them got wise and stepped to me. This was just as Vivica, the tour package director, walked into the suite with the hotel manager. The *Federales* took my two friends to the ATM and made them withdraw $500 each. It was the last time they hit us up before we made it out of Cabo.

When we were in San Diego, it was a different story. I'd fight without hesitation and wouldn't even think about it. At least every month, Dan would piss somebody off or we would both piss somebody off. Dan would grab the check, and I would get some exercise and meet him at the car. I had a chauffeur, and he had a bodyguard.

Ranger School is around 70 consecutive training days. BUDs is over six months. You were allowed to live off base at BUDs. You were allowed home most nights and weekends. Those were the worst parts of training for me. I would have been much better off locked down on base for the six to eight months of training. The most difficult part of that training for me was being allowed to leave. Going from Sunday night to Monday morning and powering back up my mindset was the only thing that I ever hated there. I would say almost more times than not, on the weekends, I was up at a couple of my fraternity brothers' houses. On almost all those weekends, Bilzerian was my chauffeur. He was sort of like my one-man pledge class.

Half Gram is still a close fraternity brother of mine. His parents' house was in Dana Point, CA. From base, it was about an hour drive. The first time Bilzerian gave me a ride up there we stayed the weekend. There was a small get together already underway on a Saturday afternoon when we arrived. The two young women who sat in Half Gram's jacuzzi still stand out in my mind. They were both there with their respective boyfriends. Having arrived late, Bilzerian and I were the only two without a buzz on. Back then, I was well-known in many circles and enjoyed a little notoriety from time-to-time. I had not met the girls in the jacuzzi before, but they knew who I was. Being a SEAL candidate and a former porn actor did have its rewards. One of the two even called me Ronnie, my porn pseudonym. They were interested in me helping them stretch after they got out of the whirlpool. I gladly accepted their request to stretch with both. They were extremely attractive and wore tiny bikinis. Things got hands-on quickly, but things did not get that greasy.

The Dan Bilzerian you see on social media today is nothing like the steaming weenie I knew twenty years ago. Bilzerian did little more than watch and giggle. He hadn't been in the end zone once in the year I knew him. About ten minutes into our impromptu stretching clinic, the boyfriends returned from wherever the fuck they were. Half Gram's friends politely intervened. The girls had not had enough. Things got awkward when one of them yelled out loud that she loved me. Not long after that, my two yoga students were taken home. What a buzz kill! I would have liked to hook up with their ladies. Oh well.

Half Gram had acquired a quarter ounce of sour diesel, one of my all-time favorite strains. Immediately after the party guests walked out of the front door, Bilzerian pulled out a bindle of coke. That came as a complete shock to me. Until then, I had no idea that he had been a closet coke head. Suddenly, many things made sense to me regarding the last month or so. This explained all the erratic behavior, the mood swings, and reckless driving. More than a few times at the NSWC, he would disappear into a bathroom for a couple minutes and then come out in a completely different mood. He would come back hemming and hawing just to hear himself curse. I thought he was just working out his material for his first TV special. It was funny to me, but until then, I just took it at face value. Just in the week prior there were two times when we were involved in some road or roid rage. Once, Dan had cut somebody off. The car caught up to us, and the passenger brandished a large knife. The second time Bilzerian was cut off, he sped up to insult the driver who then pulled out a semi-automatic handgun and waved it at us.

Half Gram said, "Nice power move by the rookie, Gunn. You got this kid all squared away." The CD changer now played Pink Floyd's "Wish You Were Here." In all, I'd been to that house maybe twenty times. "Wish You Were Here" was on the stereo every time.

Bilzerian did the first rail. He handed the rolled-up bill to Half Gram who was smiling ear to ear.

"Howard, we need to be outta here by like noon tomorrow. I have to buy a bag of crickets and feed my lizard, Pappas. Also, we need to head down to Rosarito to get our weekly *jaringes*." That's Spanish for syringe, and Dan affectionately called them *jajingas*. Even though Bilzerian was not in training at that time, he had been on a low dose of anabolics. He said he did this to help offset the weight loss associated with being a cokehead, not to make gains.

"That is simultaneously pathetic and awesome," I yelled in between laughs at Half Gram and Bilzerian.

Half Gram laughed to the point of tears. "You did enough coke and testosterone so that they factored each other out of the equation. It is as if you did nothing at all."

"You netted zero on this cycle. Your receptor sites probably fucking hate you."

Half Gram passed the bill my way after he pulled his line.

"Yeah Howard, like you never partied on your PED cycles when you lived in the house. Do you remember when you kicked a hole through your wall when you took acid on your first cycle? I seem to remember you went to the Mousetrap during training. You used to get so messed up all the time. Schiefer told me that you even went to your lineups when you were a pledge on acid and mescaline. Who the fuck does that? I mean I could see going and doing that as a bro, but you went where nobody else would follow and pledged frying on acid. It was a good thing that nobody else tried to pull that off. You do the sketchiest shit and none of it seems to even register with you. Do you know how many lives you helped ruin when you were at USC? Other bros tried it your way and not one of them got away with it. Bilzerian, I don't want you to think that just because this guy did something, that you're supposed to give it a swing. Our fraternity brothers are taking odds on how and when Howard the Duck here is gonna die. I'm not sure about the age, but the consensus is that he will spontaneously combust. Howard, I love you, but even you've got to admit you're a mutant."

"What the hell is the Mousetrap? What's a lineup?" Dan was five years younger than me, and he reminded me of a high school freshman sitting at the senior table.

"The Mousetrap was Hollywood's finest crack house. It served blow also, though. Right on Sunset Blvd. It was down this alley and totally secluded. A bunch of us from the house used to go there after hours if we wanted to go deep. Of course, this was after Howard the Duck here stopped dealing," rattled Half Gram.

"Lineups are an activity that you attend while pledging a fraternity house. They're a lot like personnel and room inspections in BUDs."

"You guys went to a crack house?" Bilzerian inquired.

"Technically, yes, but it wasn't what you might think. It was a house that the owner-slash-pimp lived in. All the furniture had plastic covers, and there was a jukebox. There were a few hookers who served as waitresses. You could get either $50 or $100 worth of blow. Some half-wit would bring it out to you on a CD case. We never did crack there. One time we met the New Jersey Nets and hung with them." Half Gram noted.

"Did you have to do any gay shit to get into your house?"

"Nothing like that at all. Somewhere in between *Fight Club* and *Animal House*. Oh, and the Mousetrap was a classy joint," I laughed.

"Wow that's crazy," Bilzerian said in admiration.

71

"We used to go out so hard back when we were in school. Gunn, do you remember any of it?" Half Gram looked at me with eyes from 1996, the year I did not sleep.

"Of course. I remember almost everything. Sometimes I have acute retrieval failure," I chuckled. "I was too busy looking forward to ever look back, but when I sit by myself, every moment is still there. The good and the bad."

"What else did you guys get into?"

"Everything. Thanks for bringing the whiff, Bilzerian. It's much appreciated. I don't mean to come down on you, but someone has to read you the riot act about our friend the Gunn, here. I don't know how he does it."

"No worries, Half Gram. Thanks for having us up here. This place is extremely comfortable. How long have you lived here?"

"My folks bought this place back in the 50's. They're part of the original beach crew. I had it really good growing up here."

Partying in Gramsterdam was nothing new. In fact, it was one of my favorite places to partake. I had been to that house maybe twenty times since Spring of 1996. Bilzerian impersonated me impersonating John C. Reilly from *Boogie Nights*. Until about 2:00 AM, we had quite the chuckle fest in Gramsterdam. "I'm In the Mood" by Robert Plant played on the stereo as we all had a few laughs at my expense. Half

Gram ripped into me the way only my closest friends do. Bilzerian even landed a few good shots on me. They made me laugh so hard that I cried and dry heaved. When the joke is on me, I laugh harder than anyone in the room. I have been blessed with friends who never pull punches with me. My closest friends give me the hardest shots. I wouldn't have it any other way. It's been that way since I can remember. The two primary groups of friends in my sphere are my Delta Eta fraternity brothers and classmates from both of my two BUDs classes; these are two of the most hyper-abusive, hyper-masculine, and hyper-devoted groups on the planet. The rest of them are ground floor people and a few random ones that I've met along the path.

We closed it down before sunrise. Dan woke me up probably sometime around 10:30 AM or 11:00 AM and said his brother was on his way to Half Gram's. Adam showed up just before noon in Lance's car. He looked like an underage male prostitute.

He looked like he was about thirteen. This kid was not even shaving yet. This did not deter him from throwing his weight around, all 128 lbs. of it. He was wearing basketball shoes, basketball shorts, and a sleeveless V-neck hoodie. Adam wore so much jewelry that he could have given Mr. T a run for his money. He had this ring on one of his middle fingers that had a Lion's head on it that probably weighed more than one of his hands.

Half Gram and I each looked at Bilzerian's little brother, Howdy Doody Junior. Then we looked at each other and laughed out loud to the point of tears for almost two minutes. In that time, Adam yelled a pro wrestling promo worth of shit our way. All that did was make us laugh harder. All the while Dan was hard at work mixing another protein shake while he gnawed on a granola bar trying to offset last night.

"A lot of people tell me I look like somebody else. Somebody famous," Dan said invitingly.

In his best John Wayne impression, Half Gram stated, "I'll tell you who you look like. You look like Peter North minus the dick and the muscles." What a mic drop. There is no comeback to a line like that. The Bilzerians and I said goodbye to Half Gram and got on the road.

"Old school right there, boys. Turned up to eleven."

I pointed to the perfectly restored Woodie Wagon in front of the neighbor's house as we passed it on the way out of Monarch Bay. The neighbor was a much older fraternity brother of ours.

Dan and I made the short trip up there several times. Dan had a surfboard, and I used to borrow my buddy Austin's board and go with him. We sometimes surfed up there. There was a trip not long after this one when we got pulled over. Dan still had his Percocets from when got his wisdom teeth pulled. We were headed north on Pacific Coast Highway somewhere near Laguna, and Bilzerian took a left turn over a double yellow. I didn't even know that was illegal until the California Highway Patrolmen explained that to us after we were out of the car. When the officer examined Dan, he noticed that his eyes were pinned from the Percocets. He explained about his wisdom teeth as the other officer searched Dan's Jeep. I thought for sure he would find my quarter ounce of high-quality weed in my Asics in the back seat. Fortunately, he stopped looking and they issued us a warning and left us in the hotel parking lot. We grabbed a room and Dan crashed to get his eight hours. I rolled up a hog leg and went walking south on the beach under the moon and stars. We met up with Half Gram early the next day after surfing and breakfast. Not every trip up there was full of blow and hot tubs full of horny chicks, but enough to make mention. Each appearance there was a special time.

Bilzerian and I watched *Miami Vice* one night when we were hanging out in his apartment in Imperial Beach. "Out Where the Buses Don't Run" was the episode on.

"How old were you in school when *Miami Vice* originally aired on TV, Howard?" Dan inquired.

"Third grade. Dan, it was *the* show back then."

"What were your favorite episodes?"

"This is one of them. I would put 'Evan' and the 'Prodigal Son' in medal contention also. That is, if you count the 'Prodigal Son' as an episode. It was the second season premiere and was a double length episode so it may have to be classed with the three-episode pilot in the beginning before Castillo became the lieutenant."

"OK, so what about 'Evan'?"

"I remember that episode the most vividly from the original airing during my childhood. My brain associates the series with that one episode."

"Why's that?"

SPOILER ALERT

"Okay, here's my analysis. Crockett is the center of the whole thing. Remember that in the pilot episodes, Crockett's partner is on the take, and they catch him. That resulted in a hitman almost killing Crockett's wife and son. He's a cigarette smoking, Ferrari driving, supercop who lives with an alligator. Sonny Crockett's inhuman abilities to manage stress and trauma are the forces which drive the whole show. In 'Evan,' one of his old partners shows up. Evan and Crockett are not on good terms. Crockett eventually confides in Tubbs what happened to the other member of the triumvirate. It was revealed that his other partner from the academy committed suicide. At this time,

Evan left Miami PD and went deep cover as an ATF agent, and every case he worked on was a suicide job. Evan finally breaks in front of Crockett over his guilt about their dead partner. He also commits suicide by jumping in front of a bullet intended for Crockett. Evan dies in Crockett's arms. On his way out, Evan tells Crockett that it's his turn now. That was one of the last episodes of season one. After I watched that I thought it wasn't a question of if, but when, Crockett would come completely undone, bringing the series to an end with him. I had an uneasy feeling when I first watched it in 1984 sitting alone on my parents' bed. It's no different now. I was pleasantly surprised when the series didn't end with Crockett committing suicide. Shit got real for him during the pilot, and it basically never let up. He and 007 are two of my favorite characters. They are both riddled with, and propelled by, post-traumatic stress."

"Let's watch that one sometime."

"Definitely."

The whole time, we split our attention between watching the TV and watching Pappas eat his bag of crickets. After "Out Where the Buses Don't Run" was over, we watched *European Vacation*. All was quiet until Rusty had the dream about his European Tour.

"Dan, you're Rusty," I said. "Look! He's on tour but doesn't sing or play an instrument. He just wears a Members

Only jacket with his logo and walks around trying to be cool. You could be brothers."

"Yup." His face turned beet red as he smiled.

It was about a week or so later when class 233 started first phase training. The week before Hell Week, I got hurt. I one armed the high wall on the O Course and partially dislocated my shoulder. You sometimes hear about guys getting so strong on roids that they break themselves. Looking back, most of what I did was drenched in hubris. In hindsight, I should have waited to start juicing again until after completing Hell Week. I didn't know it at the time, but this was the beginning of the end for me there. It caused me to miss more than ten minutes of training, so I was rolled back to fourth phase in Class 234.

As usual, on the weekend before I started with 234, Dan and I went south of the border as usual.

"*Jaringas, jaringas, jaringas*, we need to get our weekly *jaringas*," Dan said, sounding like Beavis from *Beavis and Butt-Head* as we drove south into Rosarito.

On that same day, I brought Bilzerian to meet my friend D Day. He is another fraternity brother from USC. A quintessential throttle junkie. He was my conduit to the Inland Empire. D Day had a tachometer in his brain. About a year prior, he was out in the desert with his high school friends. They had been up a couple of days on a bender. At some point, D Day was completely out of his mind but was determined to jump off something the size of a three-story house. Well, he stuck the landing; however, he also sustained several stress fractures on his spine and had to take an incomplete for the semester in college because he broke his back. When I first brought Bilzerian up there, D Day was in the middle of a six-year bender that had been interrupted by two back surgeries. That was more than cause to have the medicine cabinet full.

Living with him was May Day, another brother from the Delta Eta house. May Day was a real gem, a Masshole Chowderhead to the core. He went to a prep school with a hardcore football program. He was one of the stars there. They were ranked in the top 25 nationally while he was there. May Day and one of his teammates were the two reasons that there was random drug testing in Massachusetts prep school football. May Day was a freak, too. I believe he said he was box squatting with 700+ pounds as a 15 or 16-year-old and could have played middle linebacker in division one.

At this point, I think they were both six- or seven-year juniors or seniors in college and were trying to graduate by this point. They were like Goose in *Top Gun* when he has a heart-to-heart with Maverick. "When I got here all I wanted was that trophy. Now I just hope we graduate."

Like I said before, Dan Bilzerian was not the Dan Bilzerian you now know. I think he went to sleep at ten at night the first time we were up there. He complained that he needed his eight hours of sleep. I gave him the spare bedroom to silence him. Bilzerian was kind of a closet cokehead, and he did not smoke pot because he was worried that it would lower his testosterone levels. He was not much of a drinker. Mayday, D Day, and I did not share in those same limitations at that time. They busted out a balloon of tar heroin, a bottle of Xanax, and some blow. We got busy with that sampler platter for about a half hour and let things take hold. D Day wanted to take me for a ride in his Chevelle. He did not really partake other than maybe an IPA. This car had about 870 horsepower. Zero to sixty in 2.3 seconds. It got less than three miles per gallon. This car made the one Iggy Pop ranted about in the White Zombie song "Black Sunshine" seem like a golf cart. For some reason, Mayday was not interested, and he wanted to watch select parts of *Goodfellas* and maybe *The Doors* while we went out.

"Hey H, is it past your sidekick's bedtime already? What is it with that kid Bilzerian? I know you guys are pals, but he hasn't exactly had a strong showing so far. You're gonna tell me that this is a guy who's going to protect our freedom and stay awake after 10?"

Bilzerian could be snorting a line off Mother Theresa's tits, and he would still bail on her to get his eight hours of sleep. Mind you, I had just washed down a handful of Xanax with an IPA. Then, I took a couple of puffs of tar heroin and blew a couple of huge rails before we got into that car. We were at a stoplight when suddenly a California Highway Patrol car pulled up next to us at the light. Both officers looked over towards our car and gave us the thumbs up. They nodded their heads in approval. They encouraged D Day to rev the engine, so he obliged them. Both Sheriffs cheered out loud. Then when the light turned green, they turned their lights on and just floored it while we sat there for a second or two. D Day drove slowly for a few blocks just to make sure that the coast was clear, then he brought us to a straightaway. D Day looked over to me and just laughed as he said, "Hold on, H." He jumped on the gas. That car could beat a Tomcat off a carrier deck. Before I was able to take a complete breath, that machine was at well over 100 miles an hour in second gear. At that point, D Day's foot was off the gas, and we slowed back down to subsonic speed. Shortly after that, we brought the Chevelle back to his house and put it in the garage. We settled in for the night with a couple more rounds of tar and blow. For some reason, heroin never put its hooks in me. I used it only with good friends and on special occasions.

I may have brought Bilzerian up to D Day's half a dozen times, or more. Some of those weekends were wilder than others. On one of them, I had my first Mr. Bitchin encounter, or so I thought. It was already after hours as I sat in the jacuzzi with altered senses. A few older bros were out at this one. Phantom Punch and Lightning were both there. I met up with those guys in July in New York City. We were reminiscing how Phantom Punch got into six fights on his first day and won only one of them. A group of late arrivals walked in and things picked back up again. This crew came from the pro soccer game in LA. One of the guys wore most of his soccer uniform. He had on a red AIG DC United jersey, socks, and indoor soccer flats. He also had on a pair of Abercrombie cargo shorts. He seemed harmless enough. Everybody else was relaxing or sketching. This guy started in on Phantom Punch and Lightning about how he could be a pro soccer player and was the best athlete on the planet. I heard every tenth word this guy said, and listening to him, you'd have thought he was talking about Pele. Phantom Punch just wanted to be left alone long enough to smoke some H and snort some blow. After a few minutes Lightning called out to me, "Howard, you need to dry off and put your sneakers on. Mr. Bitchin here is openly challenging the party to sprints. How about playing party emissary and shutting this guy up?"

"Seriously?" I screamed into the house.

"Yeah, bro. This guy's killing the vibe."

"Two minutes."

I jumped out of the jacuzzi and headed to the bathroom with dry shorts in hand. I walked calmly out after hanging my wet trunks in the shower over to where my brothers were. I chopped and blew a nice sized line of blow from their package and tied my shoes. I walked out the front door towards the well-lit street. Suddenly, Mr. Bitchin was full of excuses, so the race was off. I won by forfeit and the AIG jersey wearing weenie disappeared into the night. If that guy were any more of a power tool, he would have DeWalt stenciled on his chest. Until then, Mr. Bitchin was just an urban myth. The real Mr. Bitchin was some dude Lightning knows. He married the first pro wrestling diva. It is a title of honor or an insult depending on the person and situation.

Bilzerian and I headed back down to San Diego and got back into our routine on Sunday. I think it was the next weekend that Bilzerian's cousin Erich flew out from Minnesota to stay with him for a week. Erich looked like the character Bubbles from *Trailer Park Boys*, although he did not wear child molester glasses and was on testosterone. At one point, he was also a Navy SEAL candidate but somehow got sent to the Fleet. He opted for a psych discharge rather than finish a cruise. He had a nasty case of acid reflux and was always clearing his throat very loudly. His sense of humor made him one of the funniest individuals I have ever met. He had also just undergone gynecomastia removal surgery. He had recently been on a robust cycle and did not take an estrogen blocker. He opted for the surgery and remarked it wasn't that bad. He was back to doing light arm work in the gym within about a week. Prior to his surgery, he tried Clenbuterol with DMSO locally on the abdominal heads of his pecs. I had heard similar methods discussed by top bodybuilders at the Mecca in Venice back in the day, such as crushing up Clenbuterol tablets and rubbing them on to their abdomens and lower pecs for spot fat removal. According to Erich, it was not a valid gyno removal technique.

After heading down to Mexico to get our *jaringas*, we went out in San Diego to the Gaslamp District to meet some girls. I happened upon three girls who looked like the models in the Robert Palmer videos from the *Riptide* album in 1985. They were sisters. They were 100% Mexican and barely spoke a lick of English. They looked like tan angels with ponytails. They were dressed like models. Although they were not drinkers or partiers, they looked like they were in a cartel family. I'm guessing that each of their outfits probably cost at least $25,000 from head to toe. Looking as good as they did, I assumed that their lifestyle was paid in full by pallets of cocaine. All three were gorgeous. I could tell they were all virgins. These were the kind of girls that if you were going to be with them, it was a lifetime commitment. Obviously, I went after the more spirited one, Miriam. She was the middle sister. Within minutes of trying to get her and her sisters to come back to Dan's place, she looked at me and said, "You're the kind of guy that says, 'Hey, baby. Come over here.'" That was the most English she used on the three nights I met her out.

Everybody pointed and laughed at me, and then Miriam said, "If you can do 50 one arm push-ups, we will go home with you."

I stood up from the bar stool, put my drinks down, and dropped to the floor on the spot to bust out 50 one arm push-ups to perfection. Dan and Erich applauded my efforts, but the girls still would not come home with us. Although they would not come home with us, it caused a shift in the way all three girls looked at me. That move registered very high on the *machismo* meter. We met those girls out maybe once more. If my dream were to marry a virgin Mexican princess, my search was over. This was not unlike the waitress and gator in Kenosha. Miriam was even more beautiful and even less practical. It was a fun couple of nights.

In the first week of December, Paul Bilzerian, Dan's father, came to town for his son's birthday. He flew halfway around the world with his private attorney and his bodyguard. Paul was wearing black acid washed jeans, a vintage Andre Agassi collared tennis shirt from the late 80's, and a mesh back baseball cap. He had a mustache that looked like it was a year old. Looking at him in a vacuum, one would assume this guy rented jet skis to people at Myrtle Beach. Paul was very unassuming, except for his watch. That little piece of platinum probably cost more than a Bugatti. We all headed to some golf club in La Jolla and met up in the parking lot. During the drive, it was explained to me that Garth was the attorney, and Lance was the bodyguard. In all, there were five of us. Everyone seemed friendly enough, except for Lance. He continued to smile at me after shaking hands and that continued for the entire afternoon. It was the same look some of the BUDs instructors had when sizing up a class.

We rented two golf carts for five people. Dan and I in one, and Lance and Garth in the second. I don't think that Paul ever sat in a golf cart for the entire round. Instead, he jogged to every person's shot and gave his take on what he would do if it were his shot. He knew what he was talking about and gave good advice on every stroke on the course for everybody playing. Every time I looked up, I just saw Lance sizing me up. Not knowing how to respond, I stared back at him with a smile. Dan asked if I noticed Lance sizing me up. I acknowledged it and said he was laying it on pretty thick. Was I going to have to fight Lance as part of a blood-in, blood-out ritual?

"Oh, don't mind him. This is what he does before people are welcomed around the family. He's just feeling you out to make certain you can be trusted."

After we finished the round of golf, it was off to Ruth's Chris Steak House in San Diego. Paul picked up the tab for everything that day including dinner. After dinner Dan's father, Lance, and Garth headed over to Lance's car. I thanked Paul for the round, the advice, and dinner. Then, I shook all three men's hands and wished them a pleasant evening.

Paul Bilzerian was incarcerated shortly after by the federal government. He was not charged with anything but was being held in contempt of court until he paid $300,000,000. His assets and corporate holdings were structured outside of the United States in a manner which caused him little or no tax liability. Big Brother probably hates it when eccentric CEO billionaire types beat him at his own game. When the government wants something, it usually gets it. Dan said that they were really trying to stick it to him this time. Paul Bilzerian is a man of principle. Dan said that his father ordered his family not to pay one cent.

The feds moved him around from prison to prison in rapid fashion. This was used to disrupt communication between him and his legal team. He was moved to facilities where it was not just white collar, more like maximum security. Dan said someone stepped to him, and he took care of business. He was a Vietnam Era Green Beret. He may have been trained by the legendary Michael Echanis, allegedly the first man in U.S. Special Forces to kill a goat using only psychic energy and bad intent. Dan said one of the prison gangs saw him defend himself and after offered him protection. Just about anybody would buckle like a belt in those circumstances. Just about. At some point, months into the ordeal, Dan caved in. He told me he signed over one third of his trust fund to have his father released. I think they did not speak for almost a year because of that.

The next weekend, or the weekend after that, Bilzerian and I headed up to Huntington Beach to hang out with Lance, some of his buddies, and Lance's girlfriend Trish. We met up at *chez* Lance and headed over to the Huntington Pier for raw oysters and cocktails. We hopped into Lance's Infinity and made our way to the beach.

"What are we listening to, Lance?" Dan asked impatiently.

"Dan, Howard, this is Rick Braun. You could use a few hours of contemporary jazz to get in your rhythm, rebalance, and find your *chi*. As you grow older and not necessarily up, you won't always want to listen to the hard stuff," dropped Lance.

Lance had been there and done it all many times over. I saw him as a guru, as well as a spiritual leader. He had this gentle confidence about him. Externally, he never showed any fear or anxiety about anything. If he did nothing else with his life, he would still be one of the coolest apex males I know. I bought that Rick Braun CD eventually.

"I'd rather listen to the Scorpions."

"It's not always about you Dan. You probably would have made it through training if you didn't do what you wanted and just followed the program. Remember that you wanted a sandwich off base on a duty day? They kicked you out for thinking about and doing what you wanted more than their rules," rattled Lance unwaveringly.

Holy fucking mic drop. That was not meant for my ears, but I was in the car when it was said. Dan instantly turned white and rigid. His breathing became tight and shallow. He was already sweating, and his eyes bulged as he looked over at Lance. If it wasn't for the contemporary jazz, Dan would have passed out from a panic attack. The real reason why Bilzerian got dropped from training was never discussed further in my presence, or ever again. When you have a duty day in BUDs training, you are prohibited from leaving the base for the 24-hour period unless given special permission. People did it, but if caught, it was grounds for dismissal. Getting nailed for something like that was about as bad an unforced error as testing positive for weed like I did. I was dropped from training in December of 2000. I don't think Dan has ever admitted to himself that he sabotaged his way out of 229. I was the same way for a while. Every time that I've tried to sneak up on a mirror, my reflection has always looked me dead in the eyes.

Lance's friends, Francis and Jimmy, were there when we arrived. It was not quite time for dinner, so we got six dozen raw oysters, and a round of drinks. Jimmy told one of the best stories ever about how he got kidnapped by two Playmates and a bottle of Quaaludes over a three-day weekend. Lance and his boys got around. These are the same guys who took Bilzerian and me to On Broadway. That was the hottest club in San Diego at the time. It had a long line and a $100 cover charge. One of Lance's boys whispered in the head bouncer's ear. We were ushered in immediately. Everywhere we went, that was how we got treated. Just as he finished, one of his lady friends showed up with Trish. We made short work of the oysters and had a few more rounds of drinks. Later, Half Gram met up with us in a bar just off Huntington Pier. I wound up rolling out with him. Bilzerian and Trish ended up going to a strip club. Lance disappeared until morning with his friends. I caught up with Bilzerian the next morning at Lance's, and he said that he and Trish traded shirts last night. What the fuck did that mean? Trish was on a one-way flight out of John Wayne Airport never to be seen from again, and that was that. Lance never even mentioned her ever again. Dan paved right over the incident as well. Up until that point, I thought having Lance's career would be nice. That was very distasteful what Dan did. His casual attitude about it led me to believe that he probably did something similar before. This is the classic behavior of a person who had never been told "No" about anything in his life. He was a spoiled daddy's boy who never had to answer for anything or pay full price. Maybe this was Dan's way of retaliating against Lance for letting it slip how Dan was kicked out of class 229 for leaving base and not because of stress fractures.

On several occasions, I heard Dan say how he detested stealing. He would be more likely to shoot someone rather than steal from them. Growing up in a 60,000 square foot ivory tower made it easy for Bilzerian to say such things. I do not know what Bilzerian would call what he did with Trish if he would not call it theft. Taking what is not yours sure seemed like stealing. It takes a real sense of entitlement to borrow the girlfriend of the man tasked with protecting the lives of you and your family. Much can be learned by how a person treats those who serve him. Lance was Paul's best friend growing up. It is my deduction that Paul never treated Lance that way. With relative certainty, I will say that Dan came up with that move on his own. After that happened, I saw Dan through a different lens. If he thought nothing about what he did, what else was he capable of doing behind my back? Seeing Dan reward such loyalty by treating Lance like a depreciated line item still bothers me.

Later that day, Lance took Dan and I up to his friend's place in the Pacific Palisades whose business then was selling high end fashion out of the apartment above his garage. At any given time, he had four or five dozen extremely expensive suits, shirts, and jackets that had been worn once in a Milan fashion show and then sent off to him. A lot of the stuff that we got retailed for anywhere from $3,000-$5,000 a suit, and we got it for about $200-$300. This was just the type of civilian attire that E3's in the Navy needed on shore duty. We grabbed two or three each. At this point, Dan was still experimenting with his fashion sense. He would go to the North Island Gym wearing a suit coat, a tank top, and running shorts.

Sometime in the middle of the next week, Dan and I went to go see the movie *Get Carter*. It was a remake of an early 70s movie starring Michael Caine. This version starred Sylvester Stallone and Mickey Rourke. Michael Caine was in this one also. It was entertaining but not nearly as good as the original. Ever since watching *Victory* back at St. Gregory's Soccer Camp circa 1983, I have always been a big Michael Caine fan. In the first release of *Get Carter*, Caine plays Jack, just like Stallone. The 1971 version stands up like it was directed by Sam Peckinpah. Nothing was off limits in that film. The remake looked like the battle of the middle-aged, roided out actors. Dan was most definitely on coke during the whole movie. He went to the bathroom twice and even left early. When he was in the theatre, he fidgeted the entire time. This movie marked Mickey Rourke's return.

We surfed the next weekend up in the Laguna Beach/Huntington Beach area. We sat on the beach under the warm sun. "When I get my trust fund, Howard the Duck, I'm going to have a game show on TV. I'll call it *Who Wants to Be a Bilzerian?* You'll be a recurring guest. However, it will be rigged so you never win," laughed Dan.

"Sounds about right, son of Paul."

"Ha ha. My dad said he'd give me twelve million to start a gym here."

"Do you think that's enough?"

"Probably. You're going to be the drug mule in case shit happens. You'll take the pinch," he smiled ear-to-ear.

"Sounds about right, son of somebody important."

My administrative separation hearing was held on April 3, 2001. On the previous day, I was ordered to report to the legal department. Lt. Fitzpatrick waited with another staff person when I walked in. He may as well have been the Devil. He got right down to brass tacks.

"Howard, since you have been removed from training, several of your classmates have been arrested and subsequently removed from the program as well. 234 is quite the party class. Last week, Doucet was arrested for shoplifting while high as a kite on morphine. Before that, Seabrook was arrested in Elcock's Jeep with enough crack to be charged with distribution. We are sure they are just the tip of the iceberg. The staff noticed that while you were with your class, they all seemed to like and respect you. They think that you may know more about your class than we do. We know how much you want to get back in training. We looked for you yesterday at lunch and couldn't find you. A few of your classmates in X division said you had been skipping lunch and going on long runs instead," he paused.

"Yes sir, that's correct," I replied.

"It is our opinion that the command may be able to use you. Perhaps you could find yourself back in training if you agree to help us. We cannot have a bunch of derelicts making it through training. You could help us clean up both your class and other classes here. You could inform us about those who should not be here. In return, we would look favorably at your case and recommend you be allowed back into training."

When he finished his last sentence, he and Lt. Fitzpatrick both looked over to me with the same glare. It was like they were part of this collective consciousness looking for my weakest link. He told me exactly what I wanted to hear. There is a way, and here it is. They wanted me to sell my soul and turn Judas on the guys I would have taken a bullet for. I may have been a drug addicted crazy person, but I would still bleed on the flag to keep the stripes red.

"I don't know what you're talking about sir."

That was my visceral response. I would have murdered a bus full of nuns to get back into training. I would have done just about anything, but I would not narc out my classmates. I have always had strong *omertà*. By this time, their faces went from smiling in anticipation to blank stares.

"Howard, you are dismissed," Lt. Fitzpatrick barked.

I stood up and walked out of the office.

The NSWC Command changed the rules three times regarding protocol. Originally, it was to be held on a separate base like North Island Naval Station with no SEAL or NSWC personnel. A day before, I was informed that it would likely be held at the Naval Amphibious Base across the street from the NSWC. On the morning of, I was informed that it would be held on the quarterdeck of the NSWC. Then it was explained that the board would be exclusively SEAL instructors and other staff from the training compound. Lt. Fitzpatrick was the JAG on base, and she was not the one pitted against me that day. They brought in a ringer JAG from the Marine Corps. He had been brought down from Camp Pendleton to ensure that I got completely railroaded. The command was not going to let me get back into training under any circumstances. The only person on my side in the room was Jackson the Yeoman. He was in 234 with me until he washed out due to an ankle injury. Every guy at BUDs is under a high-powered microscope. Almost nothing ever goes unnoticed in that place. It only takes one member of the cadre to not like a student at BUDs. There may have been two or three who did not care for me. My classmates felt much different about me. I had 88 character references filled out by classmates from 233 and 234. Warrant Officer Jackson was a senior instructor and almost wrote one for me as well. Another cadre member cautioned him not to. The night before I read all 88 character references. Before I finished the first, I was already crying. My JAG said little or nothing in my defense after stating that I had character references to be examined. The commander in charge of the hearing asked that they be handed over. He then ran them through an industrial paper shredder right in front of me. These hearings sometimes take all day. Even with the threats and perjury, the board members all voted for a bad conduct discharge within minutes. This was affectionately known as "the big chicken dinner." They reduced it to a general discharge with honorable conditions. That was that. I walked out of that room a more broken man than when I entered it. The last time I had a real identity was seven years prior. I was a standout lacrosse player who got benched for the second half of my senior year. At that time, no reason was given. For seven years I roamed the Earth masterless, searching for a new body. Now the one thing I settled on would never happen. As I walked towards building 618, Jackson caught up to me.

"Howard! Wait a second I gotta tell you something," he gasped.

"What's up man?" I asked.

"Hey, that Marine JAG talked to me for a few minutes after the hearing. He said everything about your hearing was in violation of the Uniform Code of Military Justice. He told me to tell you that you should sue the NSWC for several reasons. He said that he wanted to tell you himself, but he cannot. You'd be looking at millions of dollars. Just think about it. He said you even may be able to get back into training at some point."

"Thanks Jackson, I appreciate it."

I walked into the lobby of 618 and over to the pay phones. Bilzerian had ruined my cell phone when he was working out at San Clemente Island a few months ago and still had not replaced it. It was time to call home. My mother answered. "Adam what is it?"

"Hey, they just kicked me out."

"Well, I never wanted you, so I am not surprised they didn't want you either."

"That's so nice of you to say. Look, they broke several laws to kick me out. I was told that I should press charges and try to get back in and get damages."

"How would that work?"

"Well, from you, I need you to attest to my character. You know, tell them that I'm clean cut and deserving of another chance."

"No, I can't do that. I'm not going to lie for you so that you can pretend that you're not a degenerate punk."

"Boy, that's awfully nice of you to say."

"Why would you expect me to help?"

"You're my mother."

"I am not going to lie on your behalf."

I hung up then. I walked over to one of the picnic tables maybe 100 yards north. For the next hour and a half, my mind slipped into flashback mode. I sat in a catatonic state reflecting on my situation. My whole life at this time revolved around becoming a team guy. That was no longer possible for me.

I thought about the relationships that I had forged with my BUDs classmates and about how those relationships would never develop further. I was off the team. I ran through every waking moment and some of the dream states I experienced during the fourteen weeks of training I had completed. I must have cycled through those memories fifty times over.

I recalled how after being rolled back to class 234, I was ordered to stand watch on the quarter deck. Ensigns Wynn and O'Connell carried Ensign Legg on to the quarter deck. He couldn't walk. I called an ambulance for him. He had an intestinal blockage due to his appendix removal surgery some years earlier. Legg got rolled back with me into 234 and for a couple of weeks, while on light limited duty, we had the unpleasant punishment of having to eat any confiscated chewing tobacco from our classmates. Yes, Legg and I used to stand on the pool deck next to a trash can and eat tins of Kodiak and Copenhagen that instructors found on our classmates. Furthermore, Legg would go on to be my boat crew leader in class 234. The next couple of guys that got rolled back from 233 in Hell Week were Fox and Riveira. All three of those guys ended up graduating in 234.

My mind jumped to when Stokes and I were debating about how cool it would be to have a 30-inch waist, a 50-inch chest, and a 20-inch neck. He said we'd look like shaved werewolves kicking in doors. Then my mind jumped to my classmate Lively. We used to Capoeira fight and sing karaoke together in between evolutions. Lively was a guy that had already been to BUDs and had made it to third phase but got dropped. In the interim, he had done physical security for two years in Bahrain. He was a guy that I got a lot of insider tips from. He suggested that I get a box of Kotex and coat one in Vaseline. He recommended that I tape it vertically in the top of my ass crack before the grinder PT sessions. Sitting on concrete and doing calisthenics for 45 minutes straight causes a condition called "monkey butt." "Monkey butt" is when you rub all the skin raw in your ass crack. It was an uncomfortable and unfortunately common condition that was made exponentially more uncomfortable when entering the salt water.

My mind flashed back to when Bischoff and I failed our room inspection because there was lint on the outside of the windows. My experience as a BUDs candidate and the relationships I had forged with my teammates meant the entire world to me at the time. I would have gladly eaten 100 cans of dip to have been allowed to continue my training.

Dan pulled up to building 618 an hour or two later. I was still sitting on the table-top going to work on a tin of Copenhagen. Somebody told Bilzerian where I was. He came over and sat next to me on top of the picnic table.

"Was it as bad as you thought?" he asked.

"Worse." I mumbled.

"Well, what are you going to do now, Howard?"

"I've been thinking that I'm going to swim to Hawaii tonight."

"You know the scary thing is you'd probably make it, at least most of the way. Then what, swim back?"

"I wasn't planning that far ahead. I just know that I don't want to live with myself and this mistake."

"Come on man, you don't really mean that. You'll get over this."

"That may not be true. I said to myself that I would graduate or die trying. That hasn't changed man. I don't want to be here anymore. Nothing personal."

"Look Duck, I understand how upset you are. You should at least spend the rest of today thinking things through."

"This would be easier if you weren't here trying to talk me out of it. Now I guess maybe I'll live to see my brother win a national championship. He got a half scholarship to play lacrosse at Syracuse."

"There you go. You have at least a year."

"I don't want it."

After my hearing, I became completely unhinged and one of the most self-destructive animals on the planet. For the next fifteen years I was intermittently suicidal, psychotic, and delusional.

I got discharged from the Navy in mid-June 2001, about a week after class 234 graduated. They gave me a general with honorable conditions, second highest after honorable. What killed me was the re-enlistment code 4 for misconduct. I tried until 2016 to get it upgraded and get back in, but no luck. In 2012, I met a former Delta member through a friend. He gave me a strategy for sneaking back in, but his recommendations did not work.

I moved out of X division barracks and up to Ocean Beach with a couple of my classmates: Nasty Nate Albers and Auston Koth the Star Wars action figure. My third roommate was Brandy, the gnarliest female surfer I have ever met. The day I left base for the last time, I put all my uniforms in a dumpster and set them on fire.

My friend Dice managed a nearby gentlemen's club and was going to bring me on as a bouncer-slash-masseuse for the ladies. When he showed me an uncut kilo of cocaine, I changed my mind. My initial thought was, "Clear skies," but my inner voice told me I would be in prison or dead in a month. The fear of prison is what stopped me, not death. Then, I did a few weeks as a laborer, but that wasn't enough. Dan would stop by our place, usually wearing a three button Armani suit with his Hell Week Class 229 brown shirt and his fucking Birkenstocks. We watched *Big Wednesday*, *Flash Gordon*, *Bladerunner*, and *Apocalypse Now*.

Dan fed his second monitor lizard, Bodhi, mice that he had injected with anabolic steroids prior to feeding. He would shoot 100mg of Deca Durabolan into a mouse and then feed it to Bodhi. About a month before Dan left for Minnesota, Bodhi climbed into Pappas' cage and ate him. Pappas was well behaved and socialized. You could handle him, but not Bodhi. Dan intentionally kept Bodhi on edge so that he would be an aggressive monitor lizard. When he left for Minnesota and moved out of Imperial Beach, he took Bodhi to the beach and turned him loose and said he just disappeared into the underbrush. That juiced up lizard probably grew to the size of a Komodo dragon and ate illegal aliens.

Dan had been an admirer of my wardrobe and he offered to buy things from me a few times. He had been back to Lance's friend's house in the Palisades a few more times for suits since I went with him some months ago. In the year leading up to BUDs, I had acquired maybe six or eight Acapulco style shirts and shorts. It was all ornate floral print stuff, made in linen or brushed cotton. I spent maybe $2,000 on all of it. I fire-saled the whole wardrobe to Bilzerian for $500. Less for me to pack when I left for New York. I was headed to SUNY Canton which was about 15 miles from the Canadian Border in New York. There was no beach scene there. I needed the cash. He needed all the style points he could get.

Dan went on leave to his camp in Minnesota right before he went back to BUDs. I timed my drive back East so I could spend a week there. He left about a week before me.

5

CROSSLAKE, MINNESOTA
AUGUST 2001

About two weeks before I left Southern California, a few old school brothers filmed a porno at our fraternity house. I only wanted to watch and not star in, but I was given the male lead role as Captain Hot Wheels. I refused to do any hard-core stuff because I had spent the last week on a crystal meth binge. I couldn't get it up if I had a shotgun and a fistful of hundreds. The thought of being impotent on a porn shoot while being hazed ruthlessly by my closest friends did not appeal to me. When I got home after the shoot, I was still flying on crystal-meth. As I laid in bed, I had visual hallucinations of little people doing gymnastic routines on the ceiling of my bedroom.

I dove right back into the abyss on my last night in LA. It was an all-star cast. My late big brother Adrian, Lev, Lightning, D Day, Tre, and I hit Venice like a bag of wrenches that night. I left Los Angeles with ecstasy still pulsing through me thinking that federal agents were following us and hiding behind trees. D Day had confirmed my paranoia. It was not until fifteen years later that he told me he was just kidding.

When I arrived in San Francisco I continued the party. I know I saw my old roommate, "The Dark One," but I have only a few conscious memories of my visit there. From there, I drove my '96 Volkswagen Passat straight through to Crosslake, Minnesota. It was a small town north of Duluth and Brainerd. That was roughly a 2,300-mile trip that I did alone in about 27 hours averaging almost 90 miles per hour. Bilzerian's first cousin Erich lived in Crosslake. Right when I left San Francisco, I took six Yellow Jackets. Those nasty things are over-the-counter trucker speed pills. I smelled like a meth lab when I got to Crosslake. I had to cut the socks I was wearing off with a pair of scissors and pull parts of them out with tweezers from the soles of my feet. I felt like I was shot out of a cannon when I landed there. It felt like I had just driven the Le Mans by myself without a relief driver.

We were in a bar within 15 or 20 minutes of my arrival. We quickly started off with a couple of shots of tequila, and for no reason, I picked up a barstool and threw it Bobby Knight style. Dan pointed out that I needed to pump the brakes and that the road trip was over. For the next few hours, I decompressed with my friends.

I woke up the next morning and heard Erich fussing in the next room. He hemmed and hawed about what was left of a half-pound of mersh weed. He'd reached his breaking point for removing stems and seeds from it and willed it to me. I graciously accepted what was at least four ounces remaining. He handed me the bag and his rolling papers. He was heading out to his farmhouse about ten minutes away, and I got to de-stemming and de-seeding my prize. After a little over an hour, I had the whole bag cleaned up. Then, I rolled it all into about forty hog legs. I smoked every one of them in the next day and a half.

They also had two Jet Skis. Dan and Erich were the roughest water ski drivers I have ever encountered. They drove the boat in a manner to punish the towee into letting go or falling. During a tubing war, I jumped from one tube to another and landed in a manner that dislocated my left shoulder. After that run, I got dropped off at the dock and was handed a full bottle of Aleve and Johnny Walker Red Label Scotch. The guys went back out onto the lake to have at least another hour of water sports. During that time, I took enough Aleve to shut down a liver and drank the entire liter of Scotch. As I watched them from the dock, I realized just how rough we played. Erich was driving the boat and Dan was in a tube. Erich brought the inner tube within fifteen feet from the tip of the dock and that was going sixty miles an hour one way and taking a sharp turn and cracking the whip. If Dan had been unlucky enough to cut and edge or let go, he would've skipped like a flat stone right into the beams of the dock and died from internal injuries shortly after, if not on impact.

Ten years prior to that in 1991, I did the same thing. This was pre-driver's license days when I was fifteen, back when drinking a six pack and getting to third base meant something. I had a friend named Emily whose family owned an island in the middle of a nearby lake. She would drive the boat over sixty when she took me skiing. I used to run from the bow and jump off the inboard engine in the stern at faster than 65. It tickled as I skipped like a flat stone for hundreds of yards over the water. Those were good times, simpler ones. The way Dan and Erich drove the boat reminded me of Lake George in 1991. For a few minutes, I imagined returning to that age and doing things differently.

It was at that point that I also recalled how last night ended. Dan and his brother got into an argument over whether a girl could get pregnant or not by having anal sex. This became a very heated debate, and it consumed the entire day. Each Bilzerian brother said something more ludicrous than the other. It eventually got violent and Cousin Erich had to separate them. Both brothers agreed to settle the dispute by going down to the town park rec center and doing wind sprints for money on the tennis courts at like three in the morning. Right before that, Dan and I linked up with one of his high school sweethearts that was living up there. She was engaged and was not too happy with the other guy that particular night. Bilzerian got lucky, I thought.

The night before, I was with this beautiful Apache-Italian girl. We were out at Erich's farmhouse, and we sat in my Volkswagen Passat in the driveway. While making out, I noticed she had a Ranger tab tattooed on her left arm. There were initials under the insignia. It turned out that her father, the Ranger, shot himself in the head a couple years ago. She told me this a couple of minutes after I told her I did not feel like living anymore, and I thought I might want to kill myself before I got to New York. She burst into tears instantly. She then asked me to take her back to her friend Tiffany's house. During that drive she sobbed about how selfish her dad was for leaving and what an asshole I turned out to be. I felt awful because she seemed really into me, equal or more than I was into her. That was one of my most shameful moments in my life. It ranks up there with being too coked up to attend my brother's graduation and getting cut off by my primary care doctor. Oh yes, leaving a profanity-soaked message while blacked out on Devil's Springs Vodka requesting pain killers from my primary care physician-slash-cousin is a bad fucking idea. I do not know who the target consumer base is for Devil's Springs, but they sure had me pegged. "Devil's Springs. After only two drinks, you will wake up on your own floor, hopefully. There will be broken furniture and

109

blood on the walls. Do you want to really know whose blood it was? Devil's Springs Vodka."

She got out of my car without saying goodbye. I never saw her again. I drove back to Erich's farmhouse hating myself more than ever. I was really spiraling downward now.

Dan and I sat on the sofa together and he pulled out a Tech Nine semi-automatic weapon. He had a clip loaded, and a round chambered. Now he had it pointed at my forehead from across the room.

"I want to shoot you, Howard," Bilzerian raised his voice at me.

"Would you? Please do it quickly!" I meant what I said.

At that moment Erich strolled into the room. "Put the fucking gun down stupid," he yelled at his cousin realizing the gravity of the situation.

"Don't worry Erich, the firing pin's out. Go fuck off," Dan screamed, still sort of aiming for my head.

"I put it back in this afternoon. Put my gun down."

Bilzerian's face went blank when this registered to him. I did not want to live with my mistakes. I was disappointed he did not kill me. He could have gotten away with it. My family would have assumed that I got in over my head with the wrong people. That would be an open and closed issue for them. They would not have asked too many questions. They would have assumed that I got what I was looking for. Back then things were simpler. I have crawled and walked the long, hard road out of hell ever since.

I firmly believe that all guns are loaded and that the only time that you point one at a person is when you intend to kill them. If I hadn't been suicidal when this happened, I would have killed Dan with my bare hands on principal alone. Thus, this is my point: Dan is a power hungry, starved dork who points loaded guns at his friends for effect.

"Mr. Duck, what do you think of petty officer Slick Bilzerian here going back to BUDs for another go of things?" Erich snarled.

"I wish I were going with him. I would murder a school bus full of children for another try, Erich. The only thing I would not do to go back is sell my soul. Why do you think I was trying to get your cousin here to shoot me in the head? I wasn't joking around. I don't want to have to start over and reinvent myself again." I made eye contact with him and his change of facial expression was indicative of him understanding.

"Take it easy there, Duck. What do you think about putting your shoulder back now?" My shoulder was still partially dislocated.

"I'm so fucked that I forgot about my shoulder. What did you have in mind Erich?

"I thought we would tie a rope to your wrist and then to one of my dumb bells. How much weight do you suggest we use?"

"I think 40 is ideal," I guessed.

Erich walked into the other room to grab the weight. He came back in with a rope, a 15 lb. and 25 lb. dumbbell. He tied the weights together, and then stacked them on the counter. I put my hand close enough so that there was eighteen inches between ends.

"You ready?'

"Yup."

"Look the other way and I'll drop the plates from the counter. It should go right back in." He did what he promised on the third Mississippi.

We went to the bar and did lit shots of 151 and Kahlúa. The first three went down without incident. On the fourth one, I did not blow it out all the way and drank it anyway. It made me hiccup when it was going down my throat, and it shot out my nostrils and ran all over the left side of my face, chin, and neck. It quickly re-ignited. I was unaware my face was on fire at the time. I noticed some cute girls across from us, and I walked over towards them to introduce myself. Hans the bartender threw a wet towel, and it hit me in the face. It startled me, and I stepped to him. As I grabbed Hans to throw him, he yelled at me at me to look in the mirror. I could see my face was still kind of smoldering. I let go of him and walked outside down the dock and jumped into the lake. I lost one of my Rainbow flip-flops in the process. I climbed up the dock and walked back into the bar. I was not about to let my face being on fire stop me from talking to those three girls across the way. It took about five seconds before I realized they did not want any part of me. The whole bar threw off that vibe. I assured everybody that I was okay and made my way out to my car. I backed up through the fence at the front of the bar and then put it in drive and somehow miraculously made it back to Dan's camp without further incident.

I woke up in the middle of the night and vomited pure bile after the first few heaves. I could not find my wallet. There was no juice, Gatorade, or soda in the refrigerator. I was sick of drinking water just to throw up and needed something to break up the monotony. I woke up Erich and asked him for his keys so I could get some change out of the center console in his truck. On the dock a couple hundred yards away was a soda machine. I made that uncomfortable walk to that soda machine three or four times before anybody else woke up. It felt better throwing up root beer instead of tap water.

It was the morning of August 5, 2001. Dan had to report to Coronado on the sixth. His flight was later today. A portion of my face and neck melted the night before. I drove to a pharmacy and got a big tube of vitamin A and D ointment. I was barely conscious when I got back to the camp, and it was probably about 10:30 in the morning. For about the next hour or so, I sat around with Dan, Adam, and Erich and dry heaved every fifteen minutes in the bathroom. Then, time ran out. Dan had to make his flight. We all shook hands and wished each other good luck. I had nowhere left to go except home. I had used up all my timeouts. Driving 1,100 miles with alcohol poisoning and a third of my face burned off was one of the most unpleasant experiences of my life. Besides the Gatorades to drink, I had two other bottles in the car: one for pissing and one for puking. Every time I threw up, I rubbed a handful of the Vitamin A & D Ointment onto my charred face. At some point in Ohio, I pulled into a motel and got a room. The alcohol poisoning and four Yellow Jackets made me twitch too much to fall asleep. I then took a hot bath and just dry heaved all over myself and had goosebumps. After, I laid out on the freshly made bed, turned on the TV, and I watched a local air show. Somebody had a PT Cruiser that they had equipped with a jet engine in the back and had snuck out onto one of the runways. I was so uncomfortable in my own skin at that point that I could not sleep. I got back in the car less than three hours after renting the hotel room. It was still a long drive back to New York.

6

WADDINGTON, NEW YORK
AUGUST 2001

I went out with my brother, Double D, and Major my first night back in Albany. We went to a pool party where my brother's friends were. We stayed out until sunrise, and I recounted everything that had happened to me in the past year. My friendship with Dan and our exploits were discussed for the first time with my friends from back home. With my parents recently divorced, my dad had decided to finally move out of the house into Albany's version of Melrose Place. My mother would not allow me to stay in the house, so I spent a few nights with my dad. Then, I loaded all my stuff into my brother Joel's Tahoe and my Passat. Joel, my friend Chris, and I made the 200-mile drive north to Waddington. My grandparents still had a house there, but it was not inhabited, but fully furnished. We unpacked and spent the afternoon driving golf balls into the St. Lawrence River from our backyard and smoking weed while listening to Pink Floyd's "Division Bell." Joel would be moving out to Syracuse in a week, so they left at sundown. There I was, an outsider in a town where the park was named after my grandfather. That house was twenty miles from nowhere. I spent the next twenty-two months alone attending college.

All I had was a 13-inch Sony T.V./VCR combo with a copy of *Predator* and no cable. Those two years up there were the worst of my life.

My grandparents' house had a rotary dial phone on the second floor. Dan and I spoke often, and when we did, I would sit on the back side of the house facing the river, imagining being back in training.

I got back into school up on the Canadian border when I moved back to New York. I probably should have been institutionalized instead. Bilzerian and I kept in touch. He told me that he gained eighteen pounds during first phase. He was taking at least five IU's of HGH per day. That was more than enough to make his hands tingle and elbows hurt. The stack was Equipoise, Testosterone, and Deca. Dan said during PT once day during class 238 Commander Zinke, the commanding officer of the NSWC asked Dan if he was on steroids. Dan denied it, but Zinke said he knew what the deal was and that he didn't bench 465 pounds naturally without help. He bragged about eating ten times a day. Things seemed to be going well for him. He made it through Hell Week and the rest of first phase. I lived vicariously through him then. Cow college was two of the hardest years in my life. I was in the best shape of my life. I was so delusional that I thought the NSWC would call and ask me back into training. For several months, I ran over 100 miles a week. I could have trained with Dean Karnazes at that point. I could run a sub ten-minute two mile most days. All I wanted was to outrun myself up at Canton. Then, came the day when Dan called and told me he got dropped like two days prior to graduation. I knew he got dropped before he told me. He spoke with the voice of a man who had just truly broken. I knew what it felt like to sound that way. The unmistakable sound of his incoherent rambling confirmed what I thought. Bilzerian was completely shot. He spent far more time in the program than me. He was never the same. What a shame. I was still a suicidal mess over a year after I got the boot. It was easy to relate to where he was mentally. That training is over six months. It takes much less than a bad day to have it all go away forever. That school is one of the most unforgiving places.

Dan said that he fell asleep and missed a muster when on San Clemente Island in third phase. I think the enlisted mafia helped with this. At that point in training, the class is small and everybody knows what and where everyone else is. It is my opinion that his class intentionally allowed him to miss muster so he would be dropped. Prior to this, when he was with class 229, he said they didn't want him because he was on his own program. They tried to beat him out of Hell Week unsuccessfully in 229. I can only speculate that class 238 felt the same way.

The few friends I had up at St. Lawrence were all graduating in May 2003. It was already desolate up there. Without any friends, it would have been unbearable. There was not much of a job market other than law enforcement. In Spring 2002, I started searching for a commercial fishing job.

7

KODIAK, ALASKA
MAY 2003

I eventually found a spot on a boat for a deck hand because somebody had died. I couldn't get up to Homer, Alaska fast enough to fill the spot so I got passed over that season. In spring of 2003, I connected with my father's law partner's cousin's neighbor's boyfriend. He ultimately was my skipper. That guy was crazier than Captain Ahab in *Moby Dick*. The five months on that boat were some of the most exciting times I've ever had. I had to sew my finger back together with wax dental floss my first day on the vessel. At one point we ran over the prop with a rope. I volunteered and dove into the 45-degree water in a pair of swim trunks with a meat cleaver to cut the rope from the prop. While I was working under the boat, a killer whale swam up to me to say "Hi". For a moment its eyes met mine, and I thought that moment was going to last forever. How beautifully terrifying that was. The universe had put up one last posted sign before I went too far. I almost went into shock underwater when I saw it, and when I got back on deck, I shook uncontrollably for two hours. That experience scared me straight for a while. Other than my eventual "suicide" some years later, this was the most insane "freefalling without a chute" moment in my life.

I worked as a deckhand and a cook on a 54-foot salmon fishing vessel for about five months. We were out to sea for months at a time. The only times that we didn't fish were if the waves were bigger than 25 feet, when we had mechanical failures that we were fixing in dry dock, and during the funeral of my co-worker's brother. We had virtually no contact with the outside world and the lower 48. There was a satellite phone in the wheelhouse. I made calls to a handful of people, with Dan being one of them.

At the conclusion of the salmon run, I was offered a half share job on a crab boat for the upcoming season. The salmon season took 35 pounds off my frame and most of that was muscle. I was too beat up and declined the job. It took me three years to build myself up naturally at the gym. I had gone from 215 and jacked to 177 with a spare tire. My body looked like it had just finished Ranger training. It was months before I could even curl a 25-pound dumbbell. After that season, I felt like my body had been sold for $30,000 at a pawn shop. It was a good thing that I passed on the crabbing job because the boat sank the night before the season started. The crew got rescued just in the nick of time.

8

ALBANY, NY
OCTOBER 2003

In October 2003, I moved back to Albany from Alaska. I was now allowed in the house by my mom. I used some of the money I made in Alaska to pay for a mini semester at Hudson Valley Community College. It was the only 4.0 semester that I earned out of the 23 it took to earn my bachelor's degree.

Dan did not go back to BUDs for a third go of it. He got out of the Navy, moved back to Florida, and was living with his parents. That was when he started college at the University of Central Florida and later transferred to the University of Florida, Gainesville, where his brother Adam went.

For the next four years, Dan and I kept up with each other regularly. We'd talk once a week for an hour on the phone. We'd talk about drugs, training, weapons, and movies. Dan's brother Adam was big into poker at college and taught Dan how to play. We'd talk about tournaments he was playing in and how he was an online poker player. He'd talk about how he'd had a big win. At one point, he tried to talk me into playing online poker. I never saw any stacks of money. His father could have just as easily bought him the

$120,000 Land Rover that he was driving, but maybe he felt embarrassed to say that his dad had bought it for him. He said he was spending a lot of time at the firing range. Dan was dead serious about becoming a Black Water or Triple Canopy contractor over in the Middle East. He even tried to sell me on the idea, but my service record was not acceptable. He said that he could meet DEVGRU standards for marksmanship. Dan tried to get me to move down south on a couple occasions. It wasn't the right time.

He was never the same person after he was kicked out of BUDs. It seemed like his personality still had some holes in it. He hadn't yet broken out of his old mold. He was still searching for a new identity after being dropped from SEAL training. He was a Ronin like me, wandering masterless. If you spend years of life dedicated to becoming something and it all gets taken away, there is a huge void to be filled. This was where my hungry ghost stepped up big time. I can only assume it was the same with Dan. My bunkmate in X division attempted suicide after he realized he'd intentionally quit without realizing it during Hell Week. He did not carve himself up in the manner that would be considered a suicidal gesture. No sir, he carved himself up properly. He must have had a hundred stiches in each of his forearms. It resembled a seismograph reading during an intense earthquake. This was not an uncommon occurrence at BUDs.

9

TAMPA, FLORIDA
JANUARY 2007

Lance, the Bilzerian family fixer, called me the third week of January in 2007. He told me that Bilzerian had just suffered two heart attacks. While in the hospital, Dan asked Lance to call me and ask if I would come and spend a week or so with him. There was no salesmanship required on Lance's part to sell me on the idea. I was on a plane to Tampa within a day. Bilzerian asked for me by name.

Dan had dropped out of the University of Florida and was living in his parents' guesthouse. He played high stakes online poker tournaments. He had joined the same fraternity as his brother Adam. It was the Pike house. During my time at the University of Southern California, we used to beat on Pike mercilessly to the point that they filed for a restraining order against us. To make matters worse, I think that his house basically just let him in with one of those "instabro" programs. I am sure Adam talked Dan up before he got there. Dan called his younger brother "Nest Egg" during this time. Dan's brother, Adam, was essentially his private banking institution. On at least one occasion that I know of, Dan had to borrow tens of thousands of dollars from Adam to cover a tournament loss. Being almost a SEAL and coming from a wealthy family was enough for Dan to never really answer as a pledge for anything. They did him a big disservice by not making him go through pledging, and I never let him hear the end of it.

I made a reservation for the next day. I packed my TRX, an Altoids container full of Zanax bars, and a couple sets of clothes into a garment bag. Bilzerian pulled up seconds after I got to the curb. He was in a new Range Rover. He hopped out, and I gave him a big hug. Then, he opened the back of the Rover so I could throw my bag in. He revealed a tricked-out assault rifle in a black zippered case. This must have been in case the Medellin Cartel was going to try to kidnap me on the way back to his parents' compound.

He had picked up that Range Rover a couple of weeks back. He had won a poker tournament, and a chunk of his winnings went into the Rover. It had a sports package and plasma TV screens in the back of the front seats. "Before we head back to my parents' do we need anything, Howard?" he asked playfully.

"Two eight balls should cover it." I looked at him and smiled. "What, too soon?"

I wasn't sure if he was back to doing coke considering the two recent heart attacks. Acquiring the two eight balls took over an hour as Dan would not vouch that I was not a cop to his dealer. I found that really insulting. Once they realized the obvious, the droid sold me two balls. We headed back to his parents' compound to the guest house where Dan, Nadine, and his cousin Erich had been staying. When I say "guest house," I mean at least 10,000 ft.^{2} There were more bedrooms and full bathrooms than I could use in a week.

The two heart attacks had Dan temporarily scared straight. He wanted nothing to do with the cocaine. More for me. Erich did a little of it. At that point, he told me that years after leaving Crosslake I was still known as the guy who burned his face off. The coke was gone within hours. A few of Dan's girlfriends came over. They were nice enough and stayed awhile. I noticed them more after they left. Go fucking figure, right? The cocaine kept me amply distracted from just about everything that first night. I woke up late the next day only to find that Dan was not at the house. His girlfriend Nadine said that he was at the plastic surgeon's office doing laser hair removal on himself.

A couple months back, Dan had gone to get laser hair removal at this office and later gave the head doctor cash which bought him the ability to use the facility on the weekends by himself. He got his ears, nose, and chin worked on the year before. Did my calling him Howdy Doody have anything to do with that? Maybe. Nadine told me to get dressed because if I went down there, Dan would do my back and shoulders.

We spent the next couple of days sleeping late and eating a lot of Honey Nut Cheerios. We also smoked copious bong hits of pot sprinkled with salvia. Dan was way off from being the guy I knew. During one session of smoking in the kitchen, he pulled out a 3 mL syringe and asked me if I would do the honors. Erich walked into the kitchen and got wise. "Hey there Dan. Don't you think you'd better lay off the program for a bit? Ya know, give yourself some time to recover from the two heart attacks? He's fucking crazier than a shithouse rat, Howard." Erich always spoke the truth.

"What is this? A little Deca, testosterone, and equipoise?" I asked.

"Something like that. Now hurry up, shoot me," barked Bilzerian.

I always found it off-putting that Bilzerian got way too excited to have me inject him. It was even worse when he used to try and do mine for me. Oddly sexual. I obliged him without judgement. No blow, but steroids are alright. We all pick our noses. It's where we wipe it that defines us as individuals. After injecting Dan, it was back to salvia-topped bong hits. When I let go on a larger hit, I looked at Bilzerian as his face morphed into a pointy-faced Joker. It closely resembled the tattoo I have on my forearm. A few minutes later my feet were back on Earth.

Dan had two semi-automatic handguns on the dining room table, and he was matching silencers to them. He was hard at work trying to figure out what side arms he would carry to Busch Gardens. Nothing screams a lack of rest and relaxation after a double heart attack like shooting anabolic steroids, smoking salvia with pot, eating some mushrooms, and bringing silenced firearms to a theme park. From that, I had deduced that Dan had never actually been in a real fist fight before. His fetish with firearms was to avoid getting punched in his newly augmented face. To his credit, Bilzerian looked less goofy. Dan has been on anabolic steroids and HGH since 2001. He has been on one long run since he started his second BUDs class. I still have a message from him where he claims to be on only 150 mg of testosterone cypionate per week and one unit of human growth hormone per day. I doubt that Bilzerian has ever been completely honest with himself. His compulsive need for approval could make him say anything. He was a charlatan who would be on 1500 mg and say he was on 150 mg.

As we waited in line for a roller coaster ride, Dan pulled up his shirt and revealed a silenced pistol. He just kind of laughed and winked at me. Then he said what his old roommate from class 229 said: "You can never be too prepared for third phase." That former roommate was the one who gave Dan the nickname Blitz. Bilzerian borrowed some of Werth's personality and mannerisms as well. Dan could never stop talking about him. Apparently, Tom had gone through BUDs training in 1988 and made it all the way to Third Phase. They dropped him at weapons practical. He came back eleven years later and was Dan's roommate in 1999. He got dropped in pool comp because they said he was uncomfortable in the water. After they told him this, he challenged the entire second phase instructor staff to underwater combat. He said would choke them all out one at a time at the bottom of the pool. He was released from the Navy on a psychiatric discharge.

One of the last things I did in Tampa was get a guided tour of both houses and the compound. It took us about an hour discounting the time we worked out in their full-size commercial grade gym. Dan, Erich, Nadine, and I even went down to the NBA regulation basketball court in the basement and shot a couple of baskets. Bilzerian even turned on the NBA regulation sized scoreboard just for shits and giggles. After about fifteen minutes of looking in secret rooms, Dan found his father. He was in a terry cloth bathrobe watching a James Bond movie. He remembered me from San Diego six years before. He was one of the first people I called when I started at Northwestern Mutual back in 2004. He asked if I was still in the insurance business. I nodded yes. He told me to keep my cards close to my vest. Smart man. I thanked him for the advice and for letting me stay at his guest house. Then, I said goodbye to everyone. I poured myself into the back of Dan's Rover, and we sped to the airport. This was the last time we were face-to-face. This may have been where our friendship ended. If so, somebody forgot to give me the memo.

10

NEWPORT BEACH, CALIFORNIA
AUGUST 2010

In August 2010, I was in a pretty good head space. I had gone almost five years without a sip of alcohol leading up to my trip to California. I ran, swam, did and taught TRX, practiced and taught yoga, and lifted weights. I also took a plethora of private lessons on Pilates, gyro tonic, Chin Na, pressure point, kali, and jeet kune do. I had even acquired a Versa Climber for my apartment. I wore out two motors under warranty on that machine. I would watch movies like *Dark Knight* from beginning to end with the resistance turned all the way up to 500 lbs. I was able to hide in exercise. I would spend sometimes 40 hours a week and do everything on that list for several hours. I was like a drunk hiding in a bottle with my training modalities. Somehow, I had transmuted all of my post-traumatic stress into a potent performance enhancing agent. The only thing that even came close to enhancing my training as much was LSD. In one month, I took 75 hits and got hyper-serious about training on it every day.

That trip was the first time I had any money since I visited Dan after his heart attacks in January of 2007. My girlfriend enabled me and gave me a free roundtrip ticket. I wanted to reconnect with some friends, do some training, and hang out on the beach. I wanted to train with Sigung Paul Vunak in Mission Viejo. He was one of the world's best Jeet Kune Do practitioners and instructors. I spoke with him on the phone about a month before the trip. He enthusiastically said yes. The lessons would be at his house. One of my fraternity brothers offered me his condo in Newport Beach. He also threw in a Ford F150 no charge. I could not have better friends. Dozens of them lived a stone's throw from where I would be.

I registered for some kite surfing lessons on Huntington Beach. It had been in my head for ten years. Bilzerian and I were at the South Bay Galleria shopping in 2000 when I was in training. We were in a store that was playing a promotional video for it. The scene where a kite surfer jumped over a wind surfer who was doing a forward flip is permanently burned into my prefrontal cortex.

I told Bilzerian about the trip right after I got Vunak's confirmation. My trip almost hit a snag the day before my flight. My upstairs neighbor got busted by the Albany County Sheriff's for drug trafficking. This kid had been smuggling drugs to his own address here from California using a private shipping company. I was headed out to study for my Series 6 Securities Exam. When I walked outside, I ran into one of my neighbor's friends. He asked if he could use my bathroom while he waited for what turned out to be 5 kg of weed and several thousand prescription pills. I thought he was waiting for my neighbor to play video games. It was not until I got back later that day from passing my exam that I was made aware of the situation. Shortly after I had left to study, the package showed up along with 11 sheriffs. Twenty minutes one way would have made me an accomplice. Timing is everything.

I made my flight, and it was on time to Orange County. My fraternity brother Paul picked me up. We stopped at his family's office quickly, and then he brought me to his condo in Newport. There, he gave me a set of keys. He did not smoke weed anymore, but I didn't go an hour without care from my brothers-in-arms. I enjoyed as much alone time on the beach as I could manage. Rarely had I experienced the quality of peace I had there.

Vunak did not disappoint. The man has talent and lineage which are without equal. What a group. ATF, Customs, Secret Service, special operations, and other instructors were all present. During the first two days, I met and trained with at least one guy from DEVGRU. I bought a high-quality video camera to record as much as possible. I wanted to have access to these memories in the future. It was also because Vunak has the fastest reflexes of any human I have ever seen in person. I had watched hundreds of his video clips before then. In those clips, he moved too fast for the human eye to track. When he got going in person, he was faster. Until then, I thought his videos had been doctored. Humans do not move like him.

Paul Vunak is not an altar boy. He trained from out of his house instead of seminars because he was easier to handle in that format. I approached him during a break.

"Sir, is there anything I can bring you on training days to make your day more pleasant? I lived out here for a few years back in the '90s. I can get you anything you want and that's our business," I winked as I said the last sentence.

He looked at me a little puzzled first. "Ohhhh I get it. Nah, man I don't party like that anymore, but we did in the '90s. How very nice of you. I do like my weed, so if you have any…"

"Say no more Sigung," I smiled back at him, "You need anything, let me know."
I was there for about ten days. I probably handed him at least a gram or two every time I was there. He was one of the most charismatic guys ever. He taught as well as he practiced. Paul is on a different level altogether. He has the eyes of a wild animal. He looks like a Daywalker vampire. Men like that look through you, not at you.

"Call me Paul. What happened to your friend?"

"I have no idea. He went dark before I got out here Paul."

"Don't worry about it, Mr. New York. We'll get you all keyed up before you leave. Please enjoy yourself when you're here."

We hit it off big time. It was probably my abrupt honesty with him that impressed him the most. I was on very good terms with him from the beginning.

It was a mellow atmosphere for combative training. Vunak played the bongo drums when we drilled and sparred.

When I was out there, I also reconnected with a lot of my fraternity brothers including Half Gram and my pledge brother "Ben Sever." An interesting sidenote: the guy who actually played Ben Sever on *Growing Pains*, Jeremy Miller, was my pledge brother's suitemate sophomore year at USC. About a dozen of us met up at an outdoor club in Santa Monica with a pool. Within five minutes, one of my fraternity brothers came over and offered me a bindle of cocaine.

"Dig in there AFH, just like old times," said Sever.

I reconnected with Justin "Over the Counter" Colvin and his brother Casey. On a different night, we went up to Sever's place in North Hollywood and he had an eight-ball waiting. The Colvins left at four in the morning, and I spent the night. The next night, Benny and I split another ball. I got another one the third night and just hid in the room and did it. After, I chugged a half a bottle of Jack Daniels to come down.

Every training day was a blast. On the last day, I got there early and skimmed through the training manual. I read the section about when he trained SEAL Team Six. Vunak was initially approached by Monty Treesize. He was the instructor who finally kicked Bilzerian out of BUDs his second time. Maybe Dan knew this and got spooked. He went dark on me for the duration of my vacation. He knew that I paid for him before I left New York. He also knew I would head out to Vegas if he got jammed up and couldn't break free from his not working.

During those unforgettable sessions at Sigung's, I made some new friends. I got some cool pictures that last night with all the guys. On the last night they filmed a webcast for the Descendants of the Master's group. Paul played the bongos and had his friend Ron play the keyboards while we trained.

After the session wound down, Paul called for me.

"Hey, Mr. New York! Come here."

Mind you, Vunak had been a hero of mine since 1990. My friend had his jeet kune do tapes, and we used to practice them in his basement. Those were the videos you needed a police background check to get.

He threw at me what appeared to be a large ball of hash. It was about an ounce, give or take. That was enough to last a month, and I had a flight home the next morning. I broke off a few little pieces and gave them to my training partners and said goodbye. The next morning, I took the rest of the hash and baked it on a piece of pound cake at 400° for fifteen minutes. After my fraternity brother dropped me at John Wayne Airport, I ate it in the bathroom before I went through the security check. When I boarded the plane, my eyes were completely bloodshot. I thought that the Air Marshals were going to arrest me before we took off. For the whole nonstop flight, I was curled up in a ball in my seat. I hid my head down in the neck of my shirt. My pulse was above 200 for the whole flight. The flight crew was happy to see me off the plane. There was still no white in my eyes when I looked in the mirror in my bathroom in Albany. I had not shaved in at least six weeks. This made me unrecognizable to my girlfriend. She walked right past me at the baggage claim. When I tapped her on the shoulder, she did not know it was me. It took over a week for the hash to run its course. I really overshot the landing on that.

During that vacation, I experienced more personal development than I had experienced in a very long time, maybe since Alaska in 2003. Too bad Dan ghosted me the entire three weeks I was out on the West Coast, but that was on him, not me. However, much I was underwhelmed and unimpressed by him pre-trip. After this, his stock was worth half of what it was before.

11

ALBANY, NEW YORK
SEPTEMBER 2011

In September of 2011, I moved my TRX training operation from the E Studio Hot to the Renzo Gracie Jiu Jitsu Academy up the street. For the next four years, I attended regular boxing and jiu jitsu classes at the studio. I was talking with one of my good friends about Bilzerian when I was teaching her TRX in the jiu jitsu studio. Lucille made a suggestion to me that made a lot of sense. It wasn't anything that I hadn't already thought of, but hearing from someone other than the board of directors in my head, it was worth examining. She theorized that perhaps Dan was triggered by me. He was trying to forget his time at BUDs, and I was too much of a reminder for him. I thanked my friend for sharing her thoughts. Later that day, I texted Dan.

"Are we still friends Dan?"

"Yeah, why?"

"Well, I thought maybe you are living in a manner to bury your unhappy past. I know how devastating not making it through BUDs is. You spent more time there than I did each time you went. I assume that your BUDs curse is as bad or worse than mine."

"We're still friends. It's just that you moved back to New York, and I'm out here. We're just doing different things man. Anyway, I think getting kicked out of BUDs may have saved my life."

"Well, if you do get to a point where you don't consider us friends, man up and tell me. Just say it."

No response. I was trying to give him a way out if that's what he wanted. From what I gathered, maybe his life wasn't worth saving.

At the end of 2015, I turned 40. For the last fifteen years, my life went from unmanageable to brutally unbearable. I had been suicidal for a large portion of that time. It was all my doing, and that was one more thing to hate myself over. I had a couple of suicidal dress rehearsals. In one of those brief moments when I wanted to ask for help, I found myself talking with Lance. He and I stayed close over the years. I even stayed with him once back in 2009. We were closer than Bilzerian and I were at that point. That doesn't say much. His ears must have been ringing because Lance's lady friend had recently tried to kill herself. She had been pronounced legally dead, but came back to life 36 hours later. Also, he recently attended a conference regarding the afterlife. It was put on by several doctors who were all at the forefront of their respective fields. He asked me to please call or text him if I could if things got worse.

"Just text me 911, and I will know what to do. Let me handle it from there." That really meant the world to me.

"Send Dan my best." We hung up, and for a few minutes, I felt like I wanted to make it another day.

Explaining true hopelessness to someone who has never experienced it is like explaining the color yellow to a person who was born blind. For longer than I care to admit, each day was a coin toss. Heads: I put on the costume and do my sentence. Tails: I kill myself. That started before I got out of high school. I was in such a dark place at that point that I was unable to think to call for help. You could have put me in an elevator with five of my closest friends, and I would not have asked for help.

In May 2016, I killed myself. I was not pronounced legally dead, but I intentionally wanted to end my life and succeeded in killing a huge part of myself that day. It was not a cry for help; I did a real number on myself trying to get out of here. There were so many reasons to do it and nothing stopping me. I washed down 2,600 mgs of Oxazepam with enough vodka to blow a .86 BAC. By my accounting, it was over four liters. As I kept the police out of the bathroom with a razor-sharp dagger, I made every attempt to decapitate myself. After three hours, I had not felt the alcohol or drugs yet, and I never did. Earlier that day I shaved the hairs off the back of my hands with the same knife, but I still could not puncture my neck. The Troy Police were the nicest, most caring officers on the planet that night. I begged them to kill me, and they did not even put cuffs on me when I finally gave up. Eight of them walked me into Samaritan Hospital and brought me to the crisis ward. After being released from the crisis ward, I was escorted to the mental health unit on the third floor. I recognized one of the nurses on the floor, and she recognized me. We knew each other from the Jiu Jitsu Academy because we boxed together. I told her that I had clients who had no idea I was in there. They would be showing up for their lessons, and I would not be there. I was not in a financial position where I could afford to lose any of them. The light above her made her look more angelic when she smiled at me. That angelic nurse took my phone out of the safe and handed it to me. She said to quickly reach out to whomever. Then, she ushered me into an empty room across from the nurse's station. She told me I had fifteen minutes. All my training clients got a message which said I had been hospitalized due to exhaustion. I was not completely dishonest. About six weeks earlier, I'd gone seventeen days without sleep. The 10 mg of Zanax didn't even make me blink at that stage. I left voicemails and texted a handful of friends. They got the whole story. Dan was on that short list. When I was released, I called and texted him, asking him to please call me. He just could not be bothered to find out why his former best friend committed suicide, or if he was doing okay. To this day, as I write this, he has never acknowledged that message.

12

The next significant exchange with Dan would be on January 19, 2017. This was the last time we spoke together on the phone. My friend Major had just picked me up at the Fort Lauderdale Airport. We were headed to his place down there in his beat-up Ford Festiva. We were in the middle of debriefing each other when my phone rang. It was a FaceTime call from Bilzerian. That was the first time anybody called me via FaceTime. For a second, I thought it was a butt dial. I answered and told him that I had just arrived in Fort Lauderdale on my first vacation in five years. I reminded him that some of us worked for a living. He wanted my help with writing his cartoon series. Of course he did. Since before his Viagra-induced heart attacks, I have only heard from Dan if he wanted something from me. I assured him that I would call him back after my vacation was over. He asked what had to happen for me to get out to Vegas and help him with his story. I told him he could fly me out there whenever. He offered to pay my way out there and help him on the cuff. Bilzerian swore up and down that he was going to have me flown out to his place. He believed his own bullshit to the extent that I should feel lucky enough to be asked by him to help with his homework. I hung up on him and his lawyers.

Major was almost in shock. He knew Bilzerian and I were tight since the night I arrived in Albany from Crosslake in August of 2001. Major must have expected me to go easier on Bilzerian because he had a Twitter account and a trust fund. I had been unimpressed with the post-BUDs Dan Bilzerian, and that never changed. I am a product of inverse nepotism. Major asked me a favor when we arrived at his house. First, he buttered me up with a couple of dabs that were 93% THC. "Howard would you please call Bilzerian back and let me be a fly on the wall?" Out came the pitch.

"Are you serious? Why?" I was confused.

"I've got you covered for the whole week you're down here. I won't get in the way. I promise. You talk down to him, and he goes along with it. You don't realize it because you're you. You are the only person who he takes any shit from, and you shit all over him. You shit right on his face. He can't stop laughing when you do, too. Howard, you are scary fucking good when it comes to dressing someone down; you have it down to a science."

It seemed to be important to Major that I call Dan. He was hosting me for a week, so I reluctantly called Bilzerian back. The dynamic of our call was of a freshman eating lunch with the seniors again. Major went on the record and said that I was the only person who ever spoke to Bilzerian in the manner I did. Too bad more people do not know Dan like I did. They would be underwhelmed as well. That conference call lasted around 75 minutes. Dan laughed hysterically at his own expense for most of the call. I had him and myself in tears several times. Major reminded me that Bilzerian swore to me up and down that he was going to have me flown out to see him. He asked when I was going to get out to Vegas. The man with a jet complained about buying me a plane ticket. He must have spent his allowance because he never mentioned gassing up his jet to come and grab me. Empty promises. Since that call ended, I have not heard back from him. All that I remember was that at the very start of the call, Dan sounded like he was taking himself way too seriously. He may have said five sentences before I took over. I cut him off with something petty, and he laughed out loud. I never gave him control of the microphone for the remainder of the call. Dan recorded that entire phone call. I hope that he puts a transcript of it in his book if he ever gets around to writing it.

I tried talking seriously with him about reverse aging peptides. I explained that peptides were safer and more effective than HGH. He wouldn't listen to a word I had to say on the subject, purely because he didn't have to. It's a shame. My information would have prevented his case of Palumboism from advancing to where it is now.

13

ALBANY, NEW YORK
JUNE 2018

In 2018, during a brief text exchange with Dan, I asked him why he doesn't hang out with his cousin Erich anymore. His response was that Eric has Asperger Syndrome. Dan stopped hanging out with his cousin Erich, a lifelong friend. Awfully judgmental considering Asperger's is a drop in the ocean compared to Bilzerian's mental health issues. Erich is one of the most entertaining people I have ever met, but my guess is that Erich called out Dan for believing too much of his own bullshit. Dan probably tried to underplay their relationship in front of some of his C-lister celebrity friends. Erich probably threw Bilzerian in his own pool or something of that nature. I asked him for Erich's contact info on multiple occasions; Dan never responded to any of my requests.

In September of 2019, I started doing some tree removal with my high school buddy Rando. He had been coming to me as a training client for a few months already. Rando asked me if I would help him get his tree business back on the grid. He had me at $500 a day and up, cash. We hustled until Halloween when Rando wanted to take a break. He was going on tour with a Grateful Dead cover band. He and I never got back to working after. I should have known something was up from the beginning. Rando had just kicked heroin before we linked up, or so I thought.

"Looks like I'm gonna have to quit smoking weed for the duration, Rando," I said to him after I agreed to work with him.

"No no. Adam you don't have to do that. Smoke as much as you want. Just don't do it around customers." That was Rando's coded way of saying "I'm not gonna stop shooting H, and I will be on it at work every day. Therefore, I don't expect you to quit weed."

It had been over eight years since I had seen D Day. We had talked about getting together for over a year at that point. I was also waiting to get the call about working outside the U.S. My friend asked me to help him design, run, and guard a large industrial marijuana farm in Haiti. It was the right time to go see D Day. I spent two weeks at his place in November 2019. He met me curbside at LAX. I gave him a bear hug and threw my bags in the back of his truck. Before I closed the passenger door, a bubbler loaded with a fresh hit was shoved towards me. We picked up right where we left off nine years ago. After about ten minutes of debriefing each other, the conversation started airing out. "H, what is up with your old friend Dan Bilzerian?"

"What are you talking about?"

"A few of my friends asked me to watch a clip of this guy who's like the next Hugh Hefner. They said his name, and I thought it was familiar. When I watched the video, I recognized him. Then, I explained how I knew him. My friends were all ears about this punk being my boy H's apprentice twenty fucking years ago."

"Oh yeah, he likes to let people know he's important."

"Don't you think he's a little over the top there, H?"

"Yeah, for a guy who's always partying and getting laid, he acts like he's never been in the end zone before. I remember the first time I drank a wine cooler and got a hand job."

"So, are you guys still tight?"

"Not at all. He mothballed our friendship years ago."

"Is he paying you any rent for your personality, swagger, and attitude? Seems like he has made a brand out of impersonating you circa 1998."

"Nope. Nothing."

"What an ungrateful prick. He wasn't anything like this back then at my house when you were at BUDs. Bilzerian was only allowed in my place because he was your boy. That tool idolized you. Bro, he was an introverted dork back then. He used you as his template to model his new self. You ought to set the record straight about him. He owes you a bunch."

151

"His whole thing only works if I don't exist."

EPILOGUE

Dan Bilzerian is the Dan Quayle of the lucky sperm club. He is equal parts the Kardashians and Kenny Powers, minus the arm. He paid his dues with his allowance money and trust fund. He is a son of somebody important (SOSI). His talent seems to be leasing expensive things and spending money he did not earn. He can probably get most people to do what he wants by giving them a T-shirt and some vape pens. I am not most people. This is not my first rodeo. It would be nice if he would give me back my personality and swagger. Take away the entourage, family money, firearms, and little else remains. Beware of men who love crowds, for they are nothing without them. He has become a parody of me at 25. His need for approval is so strong, it will kill him someday. I also have the BUDs curse and a hungry ghost inside me; I know what I speak of. He would probably have people believe that he showed up to his first poker game with nothing more than two shovels and a bag of dirt. Bilzerian was born on third base but thinks he hit a triple.

We are all overcompensating for our childhood in some form or another. I am no exception. I was not born with a personality disorder. By the time I was eight, I probably had one beaten, molested, tortured, and ignored into me. To make things even more colorful, I absorbed my twin while developing in my mother. When I was a seventeen, a Pilonidal Cyst was removed from my lumbar spine. Dr. Sampson told me it was full of baby teeth and hair. There are two of us. I am my own doppelganger. Personality disorder or not, my mood and state of being handles corners sharper than a Ferris Lawn Tractor with a zero-degree turning radius. If I feel betrayed or threatened, Dr. Jekyll and Mr. Hyde seem like fucking Teletubbies in comparison to me and my other half. I did not want all the horrors of my childhood to continue through the rest of my life. Subconsciously, I dedicated my life to not being a victim or an easy mark. From about twelve years old and on, I didn't run from anything or anyone except myself. If I were ever going to be beaten, molested, and tortured again, it would be by a dominatrix in a latex catsuit. I vowed it would not be by my mother or French teacher Mrs. Hawver. Today, at 45 years old, I don't lose sleep over anything. I have transcended my childhood, and now I am the one now who keeps people up at night.

My plexus of friends is world class and reaches far and wide. There is not a material object on the planet that I value more. Friendship goes both ways. In some cases, people make withdrawals without ever making deposits. The account becomes overdrawn and the equation becomes imbalanced. The developing and maintaining of those close bonds with those amazing people transcends all else. I have fallen from immeasurable heights and every time that I picked myself up off the floor of the abyss, it was with the help of my friends. I would like to note that the last time that I left a friend hanging, knowingly, was in February 2007. I had promised my friend Tobias that I would help him with his upcoming move. The night before, I got all coked up and drunk and stayed up until sunrise. I just pretended that I didn't know what day the move was. That ended our friendship on the spot. I've spoken to Tobias once since then, in 2010. It was at a funeral. I regret blowing off Tobias. If I could go back, I would have been there for him when I said I would.

When Dan wrote to me for information for his biography, he referred to me as his "best friend" during the time we palled around together in the late 90s-early 2000s. We used to finish each other's sentences for about three or four years. That made me realize that we weren't just summer camp friends like I thought we were. If we were just summer camp friends, I was okay with that. But the fact that he referred to me as his best friend, after largely ignoring me except for when he needed my help, offended me. Dan's concept of friendship and his treatment of ours made me feel as if I had lost perspective on life. For a moment, I felt as if my memories of my friendship with Dan were nothing more than a phantasmagoria. His text asking me for help on his book cemented all of my memories. His concept of friendship is so out of alignment with mine. He views friends as depreciating line items on a balance sheet, not as actual humans. This is a classic symptom of someone who has never been told "No" and has been given everything he's wanted without ever having to consider the cost.

Dan, if you want to do anything more than hem and haw to your paid entourage, I have a suggestion. Don't lawyer up; nut up, instead. Gas up that jet your dad rents for you. Tell your pilot to head towards Albany International Airport. When the landing gear is up, call me and let me know your ETA. When you arrive, park your jet at the Million Air Terminal. It takes less than twenty minutes for me to get to the airport. I will fight you on the tarmac. You can tape quarters to your knuckles, you can shoot your jaw up with Novocaine, or you can do a couple of lines of blow. You can even bring Floyd Mayweather to corner you. Whatever you want. Take all the drugs you want. I will bring an extra tube of Crazy Glue and some hockey tape for you. When I was thirteen, I outgrew video games and gambling for money. Gambling with my life is more my speed. Let's play for blood.

It will be a great opportunity for you to get some long-awaited personal growth. You haven't had any since you quit BUDs. I'm fine with you doing a live Instagram video so your followers can witness the spectacle. To you, I am a negative freeroll personified. I am reclaiming what is mine. You should regret not killing me in Crosslake in 2001. Your math only adds up when I am not in the equation. You are Ric Flair without the flair. You forgot to carry the one when solving the equation.

We live in a time where nothing really has meaning anymore. I'm old fashioned. I still give words like "friendship" and "loyalty" credence that most people wouldn't even fathom. I believe that's how real men conduct themselves and live their lives by. For you, words like "friendship" and "loyalty" are outdated concepts to be thrown away when they no longer serve your purpose. I could have just said nothing and just ended our friendship silently, but somebody needed to show you who's who in the zoo. That somebody, of course, is me.

Glossary of Terms

A

A School – An institution of learning wherein an enlisted sailor learns his/her job for the fleet navy. Example: Quarter master and gunner's mate.

Anadrol – One of the most powerful and toxic oral anabolic steroids with a half-life of nine and a half hours.

Androgens – A natural or synthetic steroid hormone which enhances male sex characteristics.

B

Bates Lites Boots – The footwear issued and worn during BUDs training in the late 1990s.

Bizarro – Perfect opposite. A twisted doppelganger.

Bobby Knight – College basketball coach known for holding legendary temper tantrums on the court, which included throwing chairs.

BUDs – The preliminary training sailors undergo to become a Navy SEAL. Commonly known as one of the most difficult military schools in the world with one of the highest attrition rates.

C

Canadian doubles – A term in tennis which refers to one opponent playing across from two opponents. Also, a threesome with two women.

Captain's mast – A disciplinary process initiated and carried out by the military chain of command without resorting to criminal proceeding involving the JAG corps.

Chief – A chief petty officer is a senior enlisted person, non-commissioned.

Chin Na – A part of Shaolin Kung Fu which means "hold-grip." It is made up of 72 holds divided into five subcategories which are: Separating tendons and meridians, wronging joints, gripping vital points, blocking meridians, and stopping energy. This is considered a compassionate way of fighting.

Chit – A written note one carries in the military for special privileges or allowance. A hall pass.

Clenbuterol – A prescription asthma medicine which is known to increase muscle mass and reduce body fat, although not a steroid. It prevents the body from storing energy so when you take it, you have a feeling of bleeding energy. It is the drug that all the ephedrine, caffeine, and aspirin stack compounds try to mimic.

Contract – Refers to having a guarantee in writing to be allowed to try out for special programs three times while in bootcamp. If passed, one is guaranteed an A School before going to special programs.

Cow college – A college in a very rural setting, like extreme northern New York.

D

Dan Cortez – An American actor first known for hosting the Emmy award winning show *MTV Sports* from 1992-1997.

Dan Quayle – Served as the 44th Vice President of the United States from 1989-1993 under George H.W. Bush. He did not know how to spell potato. Known for being less-than-qualified for the job.

Dane Cook – He is a substandard comedian whose career peaked around 2007.

Deca Durabolan (Deca) – An oil-based, slow acting, anabolic steroid known for its incredible ability to put on quality size and enhance recovery.

Deliverance – A 1972 award-winning film which takes a dangerous look at American back country. Directed by John Booman.

Detailer – Charged with the distribution of sailors to commands based on orders authorized.

DEVGRU – The naval special warfare development group is the modern-day SEAL Team 6. The US Navy's tier 1 unit.

Dianabol – One of the first oral steroids ever used for performance enhancing purposes. It has an active half-life of five hours.

Dimethyl Sulfoxide (DMSO) – A by-product of paper manufacturing. Easily absorbed in the skin, it is used to increase the absorption of other compounds like anabolics, anti-inflammatories, pain killers, and asthma medications through the skin. It must be used under sterile conditions to prevent any toxins from being absorbed in the skin. It is a powerful anti-inflammatory by itself so it is used in medicine to reduce the swelling and severe head injuries and interstitial paralysis.

Dive Motivator – Dive motivators begin the process of familiarization and selection of candidates for special forces training pipelines. They are the only exposure one has to special programs personnel when in bootcamp.

E

E-3 – Enlisted sailor holding the rank of seaman.

the Enlisted Mafia (E-4 Mafia) – A term for 25% of all enlisted personnel. Collectively they know more than the NCOs although having no official power or accountability.

They are everywhere and nowhere all at once. All powerful, all knowing.

Ensign – The lowest commissioned officer rank in the Navy.

Ester – It indicates how quickly a compound activates in the system and how long it stays active.

Evolution – One or any of the training exercises one must partake in and receive a passing grade to pass BUDs.

Explosive Ordinance Disposal (EOD) – A unit in the US Navy. It is the most academically demanding school the Navy has to offer. When finished, a master EOD technician is qualified to disarm any nuclear, biological, or explosive device on the planet. In the very shallow water (VSW) unit, they sometimes work with dolphins and whales.

Equipoise – A long acting, oil based, injectable anabolic steroid. Developed for horses, it is known for dramatically increasing appetite and metabolism. A quality background anabolic.

F

Finaplix – A cattle implant containing Trenbolone used to increase the weight of cattle before slaughter. See Trenbolone.

First ball in – A tennis term which means "already warmed up and ready to play," electing to not take practice serves.

G

GG Allin - Kevin Michael Allin was a punk rock cult icon who died of a heroin overdose weeks before he claimed to be preparing to commit suicide on stage in 1993.

Grinder PT – The grinder is the concrete courtyard in the Naval Special Warfare Center where PT sessions are held. Implied in the word "grinder" is the idea of grinding down men to their bare essentials and building them back up as frogman (U.S. Navy SEALs) in mind, body, and soul.

Gynecomastia – The accumulation of adipose tissue around the nipple. This often happens in a steroid cycle or post-cycle when the drug aromatizes into estrogen.

Gyrotonic – A system of exercise which includes movements from yoga, dance, gymnastics, swimming, and T'ai Chi.

H

Halotestin – Another extremely powerful and extremely toxic oral anabolic steroid. This was allegedly what Mike Tyson was cycling when he bit off Evander Holyfield's ear in 1997.

Hell Week – The third week of the first phase of training at BUDs. Over five days without sleep and constant testing of one's mental and physical limits. It typically is when most of the class attrition occurs. There are no timed evolutions, and students are allowed to eat meals for as long as they want provided everyone stays awake and does not talk.

Hog leg – A thick marijuana cigarette with a diameter wider than a finger.

Human Growth Hormone (HGH) – Typically used in conjunction with prescription testosterone as an outdated measure for anti-aging. It induces systemic growth and when used too much for too long, creates a condition called Palumboism.

Howdy Doody – An American television show staring a very goofy looking ventriloquist dummy named Howdy Doody. The dummy had floofy red hair, freckles, a big nose, chubby cheeks, and a pronounced underbite.

Hungry ghost – A concept in Vietnamese and Chinese religion representing beings being driven by intense emotional needs in an animalistic way. A bottomless pit of insatiable desires.

Hydroxycut – An ephedrine based thermogenic supplement widely used in the 1990s.

Hypogonadism – The condition where the gonads fail to function properly, leading to reduced or no sex hormone production.

I

Inland Empire – Part of Southern California inland of and adjacent to Los Angeles. It is a huge land mass that covers almost the same area as Rhode Island, Delaware, Connecticut, New Jersey, and New Hampshire collectively. It was popular for marijuana growing, lift kits on trucks, and motor cross.

J

Judge Advocate General (JAG) – The law firm of the military.

Jeet Kune Do – Translates to "way of the intercepting fist." A system of fighting pioneered by the late Bruce Lee and Dan Inosanto. No belts are awarded. It has no moves unique to it. It draws from the moves of about 90 martial arts. The longest weapons striking the nearest threat. Paul Vunak, along with Eric Paulson, are two of Inasanto's prodigies.

K

Kali-Silat – Also known as Eskrima and Arnís de Mano. This is a Filipino fighting art developed before 1521 AD. It is one of the most combative and brutal fighting arts on the planet. It often involves weapons such as sticks and knives of varying lengths, but also includes the empty hands, elbows, head-butts, knees, kicking and grappling. It is known for inflicting serious and often fatal damage as quickly as possible.

Kenny Powers – The main fictional character in HBO's show *Eastbound and Down*. He won the World Series as a relief pitcher at age 19. From there, his career steadily declined to the point where we find him applying to be a substitute gym teacher at the middle school he attended. He was one of the most toxic characters on TV and has no other redeemable qualities other than his pitching arm.

Konstantine "Dean" Karnazes – Known as "the ultra-marathon man," he is an American extreme endurance athlete with a rare medical condition which flushes lactic acid from his system. This prevents it from ever building up in his muscles. He has never had so much as a muscle cramp, even when running 350 miles in 80 hours and 44 minutes without sleep.

L

Laurabolan – An oil based injectable anabolic steroid. It is essentially watered-down Deca Durabolan. Popular for no apparent reason.

Leading petty officer (LPO) – The senior most enlisted man in a BUDs class. Usually heads up the enlisted mafia.

M

Major general – A two-star general.

Motorhead – Slang for "speed freak."

Myoplex – Made by EAS, it was a popular meal replacement shake at the turn of the millennium.

N

the Navy Cross – The Navy's second highest award, second only to the Congressional Medal of Honor. Recipients are often times awarded this medal posthumously.

Navy issued ass – A quintessentially over-sized backside.

NCO – An acronym for "non-commissioned officer," senior enlisted person.

the North Hollywood bank robbery – It occurred in 1997 and was the second largest gun battle in US history. The perpetrators wore full body armor and carried AK-47s with thousands of armor piercing rounds.

NSWC – The Naval Special Warfare Center. Located in Coronado, California. This is the training center where BUDs is held. It is adjacent to SEAL Teams 1, 3, and 5.

O

O Course – The obstacle course located at the Naval Special Warfare Center (NSWC).

Omerta – Criminal code of silence with the refusal to give evidence to law enforcement.

Oxazepam – A member of the benzodiazepine family of drugs. It is known as a sleeper. One should not drink alcohol on this due to hallucinations and suicidal behavior.

P

Palumboism – A condition first noticed on the physique of amateur bodybuilder David Palumbo. It is a condition where the limbs appear to be smaller than they are because the torso is so distended from overuse of human growth hormones.

Parabolan – A non-aromatizing, highly potent, and toxic oil-based injectable anabolic steroid. Because of the results one gets using Parabolan, this is a very coveted and hard to find drug.

Performance Enhancing Drug (PED) – An array of substances that can enhance the physique or appearance and the performance of a body. Effects can be either temporarily or permanently.

Peptides – A compound consisting of two or more amino acids linked in chain. There are hundreds of drugs in this class. These will probably be illegal by the time this book is published because of their efficacy. I have used everything from extending life expectancy to decalcifying the pineal gland and curing cancer. Peptides are widely used in medicine and industry for everything from wound healing to sweetening coffee. The fountain of youth.

Peter North – A Canadian born porn icon known for his world class stamina and hall of fame money shots. His alleged secret is eating a bunch or two of celery before performing.

Physical Training (PT) – An exercise regimen.

Point Break – Kathryn Bigelow's directorial debut about a mismatched cop duo starring Gary Busey, Keanu Reeves, and Patrick Swayze. Second only in the genre to *48 Hours*.

Pool comp – Pool comprehension is a testable evolution in the second, or dive phase, of BUDs training. Skills like ditching and donning SCUBA equipment at the bottom of a pool are tested.

Pre-load – Refers to a previously drawn syringe containing testosterone esters.

PX – A tax-free shopping exchange located on military installations.

Q

Quarter Master – A non-commissioned rank but a role related to navigation of a ship.

R

Recruit Drill Commander (RDC) – A drill instructor in the US Navy.

Rick Braun – A contemporary jazz trumpet player.

Ronin – A masterless samurai.

S

Screen test – The entrance exam to in order to qualify for SEAL training. Quantified by a timed 500-yard swim, minimum strict form push-ups, pull-ups, and sit-ups, followed by a mile and a half run in boots and pants.

Slick – That was the nickname dropped by Tone Loc which sank the ship on Tom Sizemore's character in the movie *Heat*.

Sostenon 250 – A fast and long acting oil-based injectable anabolic steroid which is comprised of four testosterone esters with an aggregate of 250 milligrams.

Sumerian – The oldest recorded written language known to man.

SWCC – An acronym for Special Warfare Combatant-Craft Crewman. A special warfare command team that operates and maintains the Navy's Special Boat Units, or SBUs. Missions are often in close support of US Navy SEALs.

T

Tachometer – Also known as a rev counter. It is an instrument that measure the rotation speed of a shaft or disk in a motorized machine. It displays the RPM on a numeric calibrated dial.

Testosterone Cypionate – A testosterone ester that lasts about seven to nine days in the system. It is the go-to drug with reference to anti-aging clinics for men, taken in conjunction with human growth hormone. Savvy users will use testosterone enanthate instead of cypionate because it has fewer side effects.

Tomcat – The Grumman F-14 Tomcat was at one time the work horse for the US Navy. IT was first used in 1970. With a max speed of 1544mph, it was developed with the experiences our pilots had against the Soviet made MIGs. It has a variable wingspan. It was made popular in the movie *Top Gun* and was retired in 2006.

Trenbolone – It is the most toxic and powerful of the anabolic/androgenic steroids. This is what I call a "relationship killing drug." The mind has little room for anything but training, sex, and violence. There are five types:

1) Trenhex (Parabolan),

2) Tren Acetate

3) Tren Enanthate

4) Water based Tren (hard to find)

5) Oral Tren

This group of drugs should be used in tandem with *Pygeum africanum* to prevent it from binding to receptors in the prostate.

Trident – The warfare designation pin earned by graduating BUDs training, jump school, and Seal Qualification Training.

TRX – Total body resistance cross-training.

U

Undesignated – Refers to a sailor who does not have a rate and who has not gone to an A School. A swabby.

W

Winstrol – A water based injectable and oral steroid. It receives high praise for quality and near permanent muscle gains without aromatizing.

X

X division – The unit where a student goes after failing out or being expelled from BUDs. Filled with many case studies much more severe than myself. Some of the cases are urban legends at this point.

Xenadrine – An ephedrine based thermogenic supplement also widely used in the 1990s.

ADAM F. HOWARD is a native of Upstate New York.

He currently lives in Saratoga County, New York.

adamfhoward.com

Facebook.com/adamfhoward

Instagram: @adamfhoward

Cover design and photography by Bill Brady Photography